TRANSPORT NUMBER 4

Vienna, 1941

MARK SCOTT

Transport Number 4

First published in Northern Ireland in 2025 by Excalibur Press

ISBN: 978-1-910728-68-0

Formatting and design by
Niamh Cooper, Excalibur Press

Published by
Excalibur Press
team@excaliburpress.co.uk
excaliburpress.co.uk
07982628911

KINDLY SUPPORTED BY
NORTHERN IRELAND
WAR MEMORIAL
MUSEUM

In memory of

Charlie Warmington

13 September 1950 - 24 November 2025.

An old friend to many,

a new friend to me.

CONTENTS

	Acknowledgments	i
	Foreword by Richard Doherty	iv
	Introduction	1
1	The Knowledge Gap	6
2	New Order	16
3	The Cardboard Suitcase	45
4	Transport Number 4	68
5	Modliborzyce - "Aktion Reinhardt	90
6	"Aktion 12"- Resistance	120
7	"U-Boote"- Proof Of Life	150
8	KZ Theresienstadt - KZ Verband	166
9	Never Again	185
	Epilogue	211
	Nominal Index	220

ACKNOWLEDGMENTS

I express my sincere gratitude to Charlie Warmington for granting me access to the research that underpinned this publication. He essentially shared his personal life with a stranger and ultimately obtained a completed work from a close friend. In a similar vein, I would like to extend my appreciation to Joyce and Andrew Warmington for their time and attention.

For one unfamiliar with Austrian archives, numerous hurdles had to be overcome in researching this work. I owe a great debt of thanks to Margaret Moore in assisting with perhaps the most difficult yet obvious aspect of my research, the translation of original handwritten documents from German to English.

I would like to thank a number of individuals for their time, patience, expertise and for their willingness to share valuable information which helped to piece together the various elements of this story. Notably the staff of the Dokumentationsarchiv Des Österreichischen Widerstandes (Documentation Centre of Austrian Resistance) in Vienna and in particular Dr. Ursula Schwarz for her interest and willingness to share her expert knowledge.

Elisa Frei MA of the KZ-Mauthausen Museum and Archive in Vienna for her efforts in securing documentary corroboration of the murders carried out at Mauthausen concentration camp in July 1941.

The Weiner Stadt und Landesarchiv (Vienna City and State Archives) for their kind permission to use original archive photography.

Israel de Vries of the Yad Vashem The World Holocaust Remembrance Centre in Jerusalem for assistance with numerous archive and database searches.
Odelia Silver and her colleagues at the Weiner Holocaust Library in London for imparting their expertise in a specific aspect of research.

Closer to home I would like to thank Ian McManus and Carole McAvoy, the head and secretary of Millisle Primary School in County Down, for permission to access and examine their Kinder archives. Similarly, Stephen Moore, head and Agnieska Rayes, secretary of Friends' School in Lisburn, County Antrim, again for allowing invaluable access to the school archives relating to the Society of Friends.

Access to the above school archives would not have been possible without the help of William Stewart and Arthur Chapman respectively, who both kindly shared their own personal knowledge and recollections of the Kessler / Warmington family.

I reached out to a number of individuals during the research of this work and I wish to extend my heartfelt thanks for their positive response to 'cold calls' and their subsequent sharing of personal and often painful memories and knowledge of family members. They include Daniel Messinger, Haifa, Israel, Stephen and Mark Hodgkin in Australia, Noa Gross from the Netherlands who was introduced to me by Sharon Dror, in Israel and Yael Hirsch, USA introduced by journalist Lars-Broder Keil in Germany.

I have to thank a number of individuals for their assistance with the technical aspects of producing this publication; Patricia Fawcett, Noel Russell and Richard Doherty for proofing and

editing this work and for the staff at Excalibur Publishing in Belfast in producing the finished article. I would also like to thank journalist and editor Franziska Meinhardt, Germany, for her interest and assistance with this project
I am indebted to the staff, council and trustees of the Northern Ireland War Memorial (NIWM) for their valuable assistance in making this publication a reality.

Finally, I would like to thank Kim Scott MBE for once more showing patience and tolerance in the extreme.

FOREWORD

By Richard Doherty, author and historian

The Second World War was the worst conflict in history and shaped the world to the extent that the term 'post-war' is still recognised immediately as referring to the years since 1945. With as many as eighty million dead from all causes, the war's cataclysmic global effects have no parallels since the Black Death of the late medieval age.

Thus, the history of the Second World War is no simple narrative. Rather it is a kaleidoscope of narratives on many different levels. There are national levels, regional and local levels, personal levels and all those varied levels that arise from a worldwide conflict that threatened to upend the order of world society. Each level is important in its own right but one that truly stands out is the attempt by Adolf Hitler's Nazi regime to wipe out the Jewish people.

That a twentieth-century government could plan and attempt such a genocide was almost unthinkable in the civilised world. And yet Hitler's regime did exactly that. It sought a 'final solution' – the destruction of the Jews. That plan led to the Holocaust and six million deaths. It brought untold horror and suffering to people across Europe. It scarred humanity. So vile was the plan that there remain some today who cannot believe that it happened – and others who refuse to believe that it happened. But it did. And it led to the deaths of individuals, of families, of entire neighbourhoods, of the Jewish populations of much of Europe. Such industrial scale murder brought with it almost unbelievable cruelty that showed just how brutal humans could be. And yet it also brought shining examples of courage and kindness that illustrate the many contradictions of human nature and the depths of decency that persisted.

In *Transport Number 4 – Vienna 1941* Mark Scott tells the

story of one family of Austrian Jews, that of much-respected journalist and broadcaster Charlie Warmington. Charlie's mother, Gertrude Kessler, the daughter of Leopold and Ernestine, had a brother, Fritz, and lived a happy life in Austria until 'Hitler came'. The family's lives changed dramatically as Jews were singled out for persecution and Ernestine and Fritz's parents sought a way to get their children out of Austria and to somewhere safer. With the help of the Society of Friends, the Quakers, they succeeded and Gertrude and Fritz made their way to a safe location that proved to be Northern Ireland. Both parents remained in Austria.

Mark Scott takes up the story from there and it is an enthralling one, through which shines both hope and pain. It is one story from the Second World War, but it is one of the many that form the kaleidoscope that is the history of that awful war. It is in understanding the kaleidoscopic nature of that history that we can come to better understand it. To Mark and Charlie, and to Charlie's Austrian family, we owe a debt that we can never appreciate fully.

Richard Doherty
Co. Londonderry

INTRODUCTION

LATE OCTOBER 2024, VIENNA, AUSTRIA.

I first met Charlie Warmington, the editor of the 'Roamer' column in the *Belfast News Letter*, in June 2024. The meeting was arranged to discuss my book *We Fought On D-Day*, which was due to be launched in Belfast and feature in one of his Roamer articles. During our conversation, I tentatively shared a particularly sensitive part of the story involving the murder of four Royal Ulster Riflemen who had been taken prisoner by an SS unit in Normandy during the Second World War. Charlie listened carefully as I expressed my concerns about unveiling a Nazi war crime, which had never been reported or written about before. He discreetly jotted down important details for his page. After a brief pause, he looked up and said, 'Mark, I have no problem with this. My mother came to Northern Ireland through the Kindertransport in 1939 with her brother. Two of my uncles were murdered by the Gestapo in Vienna for trying to assassinate Adolf Hitler. They were killed by dogs.' To say I was shocked was an understatement.

After completing the notes for his article, Charlie departed, leaving me with an obvious lingering thought as I mulled over his throwaway comment. The juxtaposition of a story about a plot to assassinate Adolf Hitler with the escape of a young girl and her brother from Vienna captivated my imagination. Over the course of the next few weeks, I pondered Charlie's words. I played them over in my mind, diligently searching the internet for plots to kill Hitler, uncovering numerous such instances but none that matched the scant information I had at my disposal.

Not long after our meeting Charlie contacted me to follow up on his newspaper article. As our conversation drew to a close, I summoned the courage to ask him outright about the events in Vienna and, importantly, if I could have an opportunity to try to unravel the story of the two uncles. To my surprise, Charlie revealed that he had already composed three emails addressed to me specifically, enquiring about the same matter but had stopped short of sending them. He had been patiently awaiting the opportune moment to send me one. We had both been unsure of each other but the barrier between us had at that moment been broken down. Unknown to either of us then so, too, had a barrier between the present and the past.

Four months later I met Charlie at Upper Queen Street in Belfast just before the 1.50am departure of the airport express bus that took us to Dublin Airport and then on a direct flight to Vienna in Austria. On arrival in the beautiful continental European city we were transferred seamlessly and efficiently into the city centre and to our hotel.

Within minutes of checking into the hotel, in an attempt to maximise the fading afternoon light, we were in a taxi being driven away from the customary tourist destinations, southward into the Simmering district on the outskirts of the city. There we discovered an unexpected piece of information that shaped the days that followed.

Upon leaving the taxi, Charlie and I walked at an apprehensive pace towards the imposing structure that dominated the skyline before us. A striking white-washed-wall-encircled Moorish building, a sight that would not have appeared out of place in a

Saharan oasis. We gradually passed the entrance gateway and, along the boundary wall of what was Austria's first crematorium and cemetery, the Feuerhalle Simmering. We skirted the edge of the large graveyard until we arrived at the site of two burial plots situated just beyond the main cemetery walls, where hundreds of cremation urns were interred.

I soon located the plot we had been searching for and began to walk its narrow pathways in search of a grave numbered 203. I quickly realised that the graves I passed lacked numerical markers. In the absence of any markings, I desperately scanned the small gravestones for a familiar name, but this proved an impossible task, with many of them showing years of wear and tear.

As I began thinking that our quest had failed in the first hours, I noticed that the final headstone of the row on which I was walking bore a small painted marker displaying the number 187. Charlie had continued towards the next plot of graves but, in an attempt to salvage what I perceived as a failing situation, I turned around and began to count the headstones from 187 until I reached the number 203. As I gazed upon the stone, fatigue and the long shadows cast by the low autumnal light played tricks in my mind. The small concrete marker, approximately eighteen inches in height, had a white marble tile affixed to it, upon the surface of which names and dates had been etched. The etched letters had been filled with black enamel paint. The entire marble face was encrusted with layers of grime accumulated through nearly eighty years of exposure to the elements, further compounded by splattered mud which had adhered to the vertical surface due to heavy rainfall splashing upwards from the exposed soil in front.

As my eyes adjusted to the font of the painted lettering, I strained and squinted to discern the word 'Kessler' etched through the layer of grime. Crouching down, I examined the headstone closely and began to make out the name 'Ernestine' and the surname 'Piekarowitz' above it. Staring at the simple yet significant names and dates, I took a moment to process the information I had just read.

'Charlie,' I called out, and he approached me, walking around the edge of the plot and along the pathway until he stopped beside me. I stood in silence, simply pointed, and we both gazed down at the grave of Ernestine Kessler, Charlie's grandmother, the details on the stone confirming my research. We had arrived at the resting place of a remarkable and courageous woman, forced to take the most extreme measures imaginable to save her own life and the lives of her children, and of an equally courageous man who selflessly risked his life to protect her from the murderous, hatred-driven Nazi regime.

Standing in silence, I looked down at the simple memorial, processing the information it finally revealed and contemplated the secrets, pain and intense fear that had led to its creation. Charlie gazed down without speaking and, after a long silence, turned and, without saying a word, made his way to a nearby cemetery water tap. He returned moments later with a soaked tissue and, kneeling before the grave, began to clean the grime from the marble tile. I stepped back to give him space, aware of this very personal moment. As I watched on, rivulets of water squeezed out of the saturated tissue and ran down the face of the gravestone. I could not help but notice, even from my safe distance, that they mirrored the tears that were streaming down Charlie's face.

The scant information inscribed on the gravestone elucidated the reason for Charlie's very existence and suggested a remarkable narrative of relentless persecution, brutal massacres on an incomprehensible industrial scale, and an unwavering human determination to endure against seemingly insurmountable odds.

As the fading sunlight guided us away from the cemetery, we returned by taxi to the vibrant lights of Vienna, the cosmopolitan European metropolis that I viewed with a newfound perspective from that moment. I realised it was a city steeped in enigmatic secrets, whose depths I was beginning to unravel, exposing the story of a past that demanded to be told, a story of terrible hatred and breathtaking heroism.

CHAPTER 1

The Knowledge Gap

Charlie Warmington was a well-known and highly-respected figure within Northern Ireland's broadcasting and journalistic circles. His journalistic career spanned five decades and encompassed a wide range of diverse aspects of the profession. He graduated from Queen's University Belfast after studying architecture before transitioning into freelance stage design, newspaper journalism and, ultimately, finding his vocation in that field.

In 1978 Charlie assumed the position of producer with the British Broadcasting Corporation (BBC) at its Broadcasting House Headquarters in Belfast. During the tumultuous period known as 'The Troubles' in Northern Ireland, when violence erupted and permeated onto the streets, Charlie's focus shifted to news and current affairs. The newsroom, operating on a twenty-four-hour basis, relied on Charlie's expertise to provide comprehensive coverage to local, national and international audiences; his contributions extended to BBC Radio Ulster, BBC Radio 4, the BBC World Service and the British Forces Broadcasting Service (BFBS).

In addition to his reporting of the conflict in Northern Ireland, he pursued part-time writing of comedy and satire for radio and theatre. His efforts were rewarded with silver and gold Sony Radio Academy awards for shows produced in the 1990s before assuming the position of Manager and Editor-in-Chief at the BBC Radio Foyle studios in Londonderry. This was followed by stints in England at the BBC's Elstree and Pebble Mill studios before he was appointed Executive Producer of Friday night television entertainment on BBC Northern Ireland.

In recent years Charlie had reduced his involvement in the high-pressure environment of television and radio broadcasting and had returned to the written word. He had published stories on travel, culture, and local history, most recently under the pseudonym the 'Roamer' in the *Belfast Newsletter.* This popular page featured his colourful narratives about Northern Ireland and its people.

Throughout his extensive and diverse career, Charlie demonstrated exceptional talent for observing and analysing the diverse aspects of people around him. He processed his observations and insights, drawing the attention of the public to both the positive and negative aspects of the human condition, often highlighting the humorous elements that might otherwise go unnoticed. In essence, Charlie embodied the roles of journalist, reporter and witness.

As a young boy, growing up in Enniskillen, Charlie became aware of his mother Gertrude's remarkable background. In contrast to all of his friends' mothers, Gertrude exhibited a distinct character. Her culinary creations, particularly her schnitzels and strudels, were exotically European, and her kitchen was adorned typically with hanging meats. Notably, her speech was characterised by a pronounced German-influenced Fermanagh accent.

Eventually, when Charlie reached the age of understanding, Gertrude opened up to him and began sharing her background. Gertrude had been born in Vienna and had been evacuated to Northern Ireland in 1939, accompanied by her younger brother, Fritz, on a *Kindertransport* train organised by The Society of Friends, commonly known as Quakers. Gertrude's maiden name was Kessler and Charlie's grandmother was Ernestine Kessler, who resided in Vienna. Gertrude recounted her upbringing in the city, attending school alongside her brother, Fritz, who was two years her junior. However, when Gertrude was 15 years old and Fritz was 13, they were compelled to leave Austria due to the German occupation and the imposition of Nazi rule.

To a young boy those events were simple and easily comprehensible. However, as Charlie matured, his mind was filled with more questions than his mother could provide answers for. A dark cloud began to form, casting an ever-expanding shadow over his family history. He vividly recalled sitting on the floor with his mother in their Enniskillen home, carefully wrapping and packaging boxes full of food items that were regularly sent to his grandmother in Vienna.

Later, as he grew older, he remembered his mother meticulously examining the faces of people who appeared in television war documentaries, particularly the renowned *World at War* series that aired in 1973. Charlie had heard terms such as *Anschluss* and *Kristallnacht* long before he was ever introduced to them in the school curriculum.

One memorable and distinct recollection he harboured was of watching a war documentary on television with his mother. At a particular point during the programme, Gertrude abruptly stood up, stamped her feet vigorously on the floor and stormed out of the room, tears streaming down her face. Startled and confused, Charlie attempted to recall the content of the screen that had triggered such a strong reaction before following her into the kitchen a few minutes later to offer her comfort. No explanation was offered by Gertrude as to what had triggered her reaction.

It was evident that throughout his childhood and into his adulthood, Charlie felt that a significant portion of his family history had been withheld from him. He felt unprepared to discuss his family's life in Vienna and was unable to comprehend the underlying reasons for his mother's outbursts. Surprisingly, he only discovered his grandfather's name, Leopold, in the late 1970s when he had established himself with a career at the BBC. However, this was all he knew, the name Leopold; but no further details about him or about Vienna.

Charlie's family enquiries were further hindered by a negative and offensive attitude towards Vienna expressed by his grandmother on his father's side. Instead of escalating the difficult family situation, Charlie made a conscious decision to refrain from probing further and allowed the family history to remain untouched for several years. He had gained sufficient knowledge to recognise that this history was deeply troubling and that his mother, Gertrude, had endured profound emotional wounds during the war without showing any outward manifestations.

Despite his inquisitive nature and professional background, he was unable to delve deeper into the reasons behind his family's experiences.

Following the passing of his grandmother in 1991, Charlie began to recognise the importance of addressing challenging questions to ensure their resolution. He commenced gradually enquiring about his family history, particularly with his mother. In June 1999, as an attempt to obtain information indirectly, he recorded an interview with his mother conducted by academic Doctor David Warn who had interviewed several Viennese Holocaust survivors in Northern Ireland. Gertrude provided all the information she possessed and her words were recorded on magnetic tape.

Although this interview served as a foundation for the narrative, it was complemented by Charlie's direct knowledge from his mother. Consequently, his understanding of the story was shaped by those sources as follows.

Gertrude Kessler was born on 10 April 1924 in Vienna, Austria. Her father was Leopold Kessler and her mother was Ernestine, her maiden name being Schrekinger. Gertrude had a younger brother named Fred, who was originally named Fritz in German and was a year-and-a-half younger than her. During her childhood Gertrude lived with her family and grandparents before moving into their own home when she was approximately six or seven years old.

Leopold worked in a slaughterhouse located at a considerable distance from Vienna city centre, resulting in long working hours, typically leaving the house early in the morning and returning late in the evening. Ernestine retained the family home. Gertrude recalled a large extended family on her mother's side and one of her father's sisters, Annie, babysat for Gertrude and Fritz.

Gertrude described their working-class background, with all family members employed by the state and all aspects of life subject to state control. She contrasted this with her later life in Northern Ireland, describing Vienna in her words as 'communistic'. Regarding religion, Gertrude had no religious practice; she and her brother co-existed with both Jews and non-Jews and enjoyed a happy childhood and school life.

However, in March 1938, as Gertrude herself stated, 'Hitler came' and things changed rapidly. Gertrude remembered vividly a Friday evening in March 1938 when planes flew over the city and dropped leaflets. German troops then entered Vienna and, on the Saturday morning, a large parade of German soldiers was cheered through the streets by the people of Vienna.

In her school, crucifixes, which had been present in each classroom, were removed and replaced with portraits of Adolf Hitler.

A few weeks passed and, at school, the children were informed that they would be joining the Hitler Youth. Gertrude and Fritz returned home brimming with enthusiasm and excitement, enthusiastically informing their parents of the opportunities presented by this newly established club. Ernestine and Leopold remained silent about this matter until after some time, approaching the point of joining, when they revealed a crucial truth to their children: they were ineligible to participate in any organisation affiliated with the Hitler Youth due to their father Leopold's Jewish heritage.

Initially, Gertrude failed to comprehend the significance of this revelation. However, she later discovered that her father had renounced Judaism at the age of 20 in 1922 and converted to Catholicism. Her mother and the majority of her family loosely adhered to Catholicism. Consequently, Gertrude questioned how this historical event could have any bearing on her life, given that it had transpired long before her birth.

The Kessler family did not adhere to any religious affiliation and did not attend church. Gertrude believed that she was devoid of religious identity at that time. However, this revelation abruptly transformed their lives. The new school to which Gertrude and Fritz had been enrolled was Jewish. The Kessler children were unfamiliar with Jewish culture and traditions and they immediately encountered difficulties. The other students in the school assumed that Gertrude and Fritz were Jewish, mirroring their own religious identity. However, the reality was that the two young Kesslers found themselves unable to cope with this unfamiliar environment. They remained passive observers, unable to participate in classroom activities.

At the same time Leopold and Ernestine Kessler came to the realisation that they had to take action to protect their children. Gertrude understood that her parents were confronted with impossible choices. She also recognised that they lacked any support, despite being labelled as Jewish. They were not supported by the Jewish Council nor by the Catholic or Protestant church structures. Gertrude recognised that the difficult situation they found themselves in could not continue indefinitely and her parents also acknowledged that drastic measures were necessary for the family's survival.

Gertrude recalled that her mother discovered that the Society of Friends in Vienna was assisting children in similar predicaments by evacuating them from Austria. She approached the Society of Friends, or Quakers, and they agreed to help evacuate her and her brother, Fritz, to a safe location. The safe location was Northern Ireland. On 26 April 1939, Gertrude and Fritz boarded a train in Vienna, accompanied by approximately two hundred other frightened and disoriented children. In one hand, she carried a small suitcase containing the food her parents could spare to sustain the children during their journey. In the other hand, she held tightly to her brother Fritz's hand, having promised her mother that she would never let go.

Ernestine and Leopold Kessler bid farewell to their children at Vienna's Westbahnhof station. Once the children boarded the train and it began to move away from the platform, Ernestine ran alongside the carriage carrying her children until she could no longer keep pace with the train. Gertrude remembered that her father, Leopold, remained in the background, concealed and reluctant to be seen. Her final recollection of her father was of a man hunted, hesitant to venture outdoors and filled with fear.

This was the extent of Gertrude's knowledge of the circumstances that led to her evacuation from Vienna and the separation from her parents and what formed the basis of Charlie's knowledge of his family's story.

Gertrude's oral history interviews, a few of which have been recorded over the years, provided Charlie with this foundation of the family narrative. He had numerous questions for which there were no answers, attempts to delve deeper into Gertrude's recollections invariably elicited tears and a lack of response from her, accompanied by a sense of guilt on his part for raising the subject. At best, Charlie was grappling with the memories of a 15-year-old girl whose family life abruptly ended in fear and tension at Westbahnhof station in Vienna on that April morning of 1939.

As the years passed, trips to Vienna with his mother did little to rekindle her memories. During a visit to a former family address at Streffleurgasse in the city, Gertrude recalled her father standing outside the entrance to apartments at number 4. She pointed to a spot on the pavement and informed Charlie that this was where her father stood holding the handle of a small cart that contained all the family's belongings. An attempt by Charlie to prompt her to elaborate on the statement was met with tears. Similarly, Gertrude hinted at a family story that she became aware of after the war. She informed Charlie that two uncles had been arrested and brutally murdered by the Gestapo for, in her words, 'attempting to assassinate Hitler'. She mentioned the existence of a photograph depicting three stones, erected as a memorial in their honour, but she was unable to provide the location or their names, only that her cousins in Vienna held them in high regard. Charlie's subsequent research into murder plots and assassination attempts against the Nazi leader, which were numerous, yielded no results.

In June 1996, during her travels, Gertrude visited Israel and made a conscious effort to visit the Yad Vashem Jewish Museum and Archives. Upon her visit, she completed a handwritten form, a page of testimony, which contained all the information she knew about her father's details. This form documented his murder during the Holocaust.

Today, the same forms can be completed online and submitted from anywhere in the world. The documents are digitised and can be viewed online for remembrance and research purposes. Charlie retained a copy of the form his mother submitted, on which Gertrude had written his grandfather's name, family details, his last address in Vienna at Streffleurgasse 4, her own details, and her address in Enniskillen, Northern Ireland.

In response to the questions on the form regarding the date and location of her father's death, Gertrude had written '1942??'

and 'In a camp in Poland'. She also attached a copy of a photograph of her father, Leopold, to the same document.

In June 2024 the author downloaded the digitised version of this document and was surprised to discover that Gertrude had not only written on the front face of the proforma but also on the blank rear of the printed sheet. The content of the text, when shown to Charlie, took an emotional toll on him. Gertrude, in block capitals, had written the following:[1]

> Description of Father: About 5 foot 10 inches tall – (1 metre 70cm) Black curly hair – quite thin – born 20 July 1902 in Vienna. He was 37 years old when in 1939 I became a refugee and was sent to Ireland with an only brother. We both married and remain British citizens. Mother died 5 years ago she never could talk what really happened to her husband, our father. If possible we would like to know, however realise it could turn out to be impossible as we know so few details and we were only children when we fled Austria.

The document was signed with one of her small, personalised adhesive address labels which added an additional layer of helplessness to the testimony. The contents of this page had remained unseen by Charlie for twenty-eight years; the revelation was devastating. For years Charlie had believed that his mother was, for some inexplicable reason, simply not telling him what she knew. He had assumed that he was somehow not qualified to hear the truth and that her silence was her prerogative, a way of protecting him from the grief and pain that she had endured for all of her adult life. The reality was stark: it was not the case that she had not told him; the fact was that she simply did not know and, in turn, her mother, Ernestine, had not told her, partly for

---

[1] Testimony of Gertrude Warmington, https://collections.yadvashem.org/en/names/13955174 accessed 11/5/2025

the same reason. The reach of the brutal Nazi regime had spanned a generation and it had metaphorically slapped Charlie in the face for having the audacity to seek the truth. That shameful truth would eventually come to light, and the story would be told. Unfortunately for Charlie it was left to him alone to process the pain of the truth that his mother had been spared. He was about to become a victim of the Shoah, a second-generation Holocaust survivor.

CHAPTER 2

New Order

At the time of Gertrude and Fritz's *Kindertransport* evacuation from Vienna on 26 April 1939, Leopold Kessler had good reason to conceal himself in the shadows of Westbahnhof station. The evacuation of his children marked the latest in a series of deprivations and humiliations he had endured since before the German occupation of Austria.

Leopold Kessler was indeed born a Jew. His father, Salomon, originated from Krakow, Poland, and relocated to Vienna, where he established a goldsmith and jewellery shop at 16 Hannovergasse in the twentieth district. Leopold apprenticed under his father, specialising in ring making upon completing his training in 1921. At approximately this juncture, Leopold perceived a growing level of anti-semitism in Vienna, which had been an undercurrent since his birth. As a non-religious individual, he seized the opportunity, shortly before marrying Ernestine, to renounce Judaism and convert to Catholicism to facilitate their marriage in a Catholic church. This conversion was documented in state archive documents dated 6 September 1922.[2] Ernestine Schrekinger and her family loosely adhered to the Catholic faith.

Following his marriage to Ernestine, Leopold changed profession and commenced working for the state in an administrative capacity at an abattoir on the outskirts of Vienna. Their two children, Gertrude and Fritz, were born in 1924 and 1926 respectively. During that period, the family resided with Ernestine's father at his Hannovergasse 19 apartment before relocating to an apartment of their own at Leystrasse 23, also situated within the twentieth district.

Leystrasse 23 was part of a newly constructed housing block, built between 1930 and 1931 in the socialist *Red Vienna* architectural style. This impressive municipal housing unit, one of many constructed during the *Red Vienna* era, provided accommodation for 389 families, offering modern amenities such as a medical centre, gardens, children's play areas, a laundry and even a communal swimming pool.

In her oral history recordings, Gertrude expressed fond memories of her time residing there and attending the nearby school situated a few hundred yards away at Stromstrasse 78. Regrettably, within a short span of time, the Kessler family's circumstances underwent a profound transformation.

The catalyst for this transformation was the three-day revolution that took place in Vienna between 12 and 15 February 1934. Violence erupted between the Social Democratic Worker's Party of Austria (SDAPÖ) and the ruling conservative Christian Socialist Party, led by Engelbert Dolfuss. Dolfuss had suspended the Austrian Parliament the preceding March following a contentious vote over railway worker's wages. However, despite this, Dolfuss continued to rule by decree, using dated 1917 emergency laws.

---

[2] Jewishgen Austria, Vienna Converts to Judaism database https://www.jewishgen.org/databases/jgdetail_2.php accessed 11/5/2025

In response to the escalating left-wing violence and the influence and infiltration of the German Nazi Party, which was then focused on all matters Austrian, Dolfuss initiated the imprisonment of known members of the Social Democratic Party and the similarly-aligned Marxist-oriented workers' movement.

On 12 February 1934 matters reached a critical juncture when police conducted a search of the headquarters of the Social Democrats in Linz. Members of the banned Republic Protection League, the paramilitary wing of the SDAPÖ, who were present in the building and armed, opened fire on the police, sparking a confrontation. This violence swiftly spread to Vienna, where the Protection League members and supporters barricaded themselves within several newly constructed and heavily fortified municipal housing blocks.

The Austrian military, along with the armed police and gendarmerie, remained steadfastly loyal to the government. Using their superior numbers and light artillery, they swiftly quelled the uprising.

The conflict resulted in significant loss of life on both sides with hundreds of individuals killed and wounded. The SDAPÖ and workers' unions were immediately outlawed and the socialist leaders were apprehended for trial. Many evaded arrest by escaping across Austria's border with Czechoslovakia; nine of the leaders were apprehended and executed by hanging.

Adolf Hitler, the German Chancellor, had been closely monitoring events in Austria since assuming power in Germany in January 1933. While the Austrian leader had suppressed the socialist uprising, his right-wing government continued to oppose the significant Nazi influence within his country. They sought to align and make peace with Mussolini's Italy, located on Austria's southern border, in an attempt to establish a more stable fascist regime based on similar Catholic ideals, which Hitler referred to as 'Austrofascism'.

Engelbert Dolfuss reacted by banning the Nazi Party within Austria, severely underestimating the ambitions of his Nazi neighbour, Adolf Hitler, and his vision for uniting all German-speaking nations under the rule of the Third Reich.

Later that year, on 25 July 1934, a group of approximately 140 Austrian Nazis, aided by their German counterparts, attempted a coup d'état in Vienna by storming the Chancellery building. They gained entry and systematically moved from room to room, taking hostages as they went until they encountered Dolfuss. He was shot twice and fatally wounded but his cabinet managed to escape.[3]

The coup was suppressed swiftly and Dolfuss was replaced as Chancellor by his Minister for Education, Kurt von Schuschnigg. Executions and prison sentences were carried out swiftly for those involved. In the ensuing months, Schuschnigg faced an arduous task in attempting to maintain control over the growing strength of the Austrian Nazis. Initially, he found solace in the support of Mussolini on his southern border but this support vanished when the Italian dictator sought and obtained assistance from Germany to aid him in the Second Italo-Ethiopian War. Faced with an ever-expanding and menacing German army encroaching upon his borders, Schuschnigg dedicated the next two years to appeasing Hitler. Ultimately, matters reached a critical juncture within a mere four weeks in 1938. On 12 February Schuschnigg met with Adolf Hitler at his Berghof retreat near Berchtesgaden in Bavaria. The purpose of the meeting was to foster diplomatic relations between the two nations but it concluded with Hitler issuing Schuschnigg with an ultimatum. In exchange for relinquishing power to the Austrian Nazis, Hitler would offer recognition of Austria's national sovereignty. Reluctantly, Schuschnigg signed an agreement that the Austrian president, Wilhelm Miklas, opposed vehemently. In an attempt to rally the Austrian political parties, Schuschnigg announced a plebiscite scheduled for 13 March 1938, during

---

[3] City of Vienna Official Communication and Media; https://www.wien.gv.at/english/history/commemoration/february-1934.html accessed 11/5/2025

which the question of Austria's independence would be presented to the populace.

To secure a significant number of votes, Schuschnigg attempted to negotiate a deal with the previously banned Social Democrats and trade unions. He agreed to legalise them in exchange for their support in the referendum. However, Hitler found this proposal unacceptable and demanded that the plebiscite be cancelled, Schuschnigg resign and that the Nazi sympathiser Arthur Seyss-Inquart be appointed in his place. Schuschnigg, effectively compelled to resign, stepped down on 11 March 1938. The following day German troops marched into Austria and were greeted by jubilant crowds.[4] These events, witnessed by the 14-year-old Gertrude Kessler, marked the beginning of the final chapter of her childhood memories.

For Gertrude's parents, particularly her father Leopold, the quality of life deteriorated rapidly. Within two days of the Nazis assuming control in what became known as the Anschluss Österreichs, Austria was annexed into the German Reich and governing power shifted from Vienna to Berlin. Vienna effectively became another city within the German Empire under Hitler's Nazi rule.

Prior to this, Gertrude and her younger brother Fritz had enjoyed a contented childhood in Vienna, akin to the experiences of most children during any historical period. Adult politics held no sway over their lives; their concerns were limited to the playground and their school friendships. Gertrude maintained a small autograph book in which she collected messages and drawings from her school friends and teachers, all indicating a harmonious social interaction. This positive school environment is reflected in her school reports which remain in the family's possession today.

---

[4] United States Holocaust Memorial Museum, Holocaust Encyclopedia online;
https://www.wien.gv.at/english/history/commemoration/february-1934.html accessed 11/5/2025

Her reports indicate that Gertrude was an exceptional student, consistently achieving excellent class results and attendance. The only period of absence recorded was a 29-day spell during her 1934/35 academic year, coinciding with the disruptions caused by the Austrian workers' uprising, which centred around her school, Stromstrasse, in the Red Vienna district.

In contrast, Leopold and Ernestine Kessler had witnessed events unfolding in neighbouring Germany that, until March 1938, may have caused them some concern but did not compel them to take drastic action in their daily lives. One significant event that they would have viewed with some apprehension was the implementation of what became known as the Nuremberg Laws in Nazi Germany. As Hitler and the Nazi Party gained popularity and eventually gained power in Germany, his anti-Semitic ideology became entrenched in German society. Since the early 1920s, Hitler had propagated his belief in 'Jewish Bolshevism', portraying the Jewish people as the adversaries of a prosperous Germany and excluding them from his concept of *Volksgemeinschaft* or German people's community. Consequently, Jews faced discrimination in all facets of German life. Within weeks of Hitler's ascent to power in January 1933 he enacted a series of discriminatory laws against the Jews, effectively segregating them from society. Jews were compelled to retire from civil service positions and all aspects of the legal profession; doctors and other professionals were barred from practice and Jews were prohibited from teaching at universities. Jewish businesses were outlawed and prohibited from engaging in trade with Aryan Germans. The legislation was enacted by the National Socialist state against the backdrop of violence against Jews with the intention of forcing the Jewish people out of Germany.

One notable public action that did not go unnoticed by the international press was a nationwide event organised by the Nazi German Student Association to 'purge by fire' any 'un-German spirit'. On the evening of 10 May 1933 large groups of university students engaged in the burning of numerous volumes of 'un-German' literature. The event in Berlin was reported in *The London Times'* 11May edition as follows:

> FROM OUR OWN CORRESPONDENT BERLIN, MAY 10 About 20,000 'Marxist," pacifist, Jewish, or other un-German' books, 'collected' by the Nazi-led students of Berlin University during recent days from public libraries and private owners, were burnt to-night in the Opera Place in Berlin in the presence of Dr Goebbels, the Minister for Propaganda. The books and periodicals included the works of Pacifists such as Ludwig Renn (particular stress is laid on this type of literature); books with an anti-war message such as Remarque's 'All Quiet on the Western Front'; histories of the World War which are Pacifist or defeatist: books criticising Signor Mussolini or Italian Fascism; all Marxist and Communist publications (including the complete works of Karl Marx and Lenin); books by Jewish authors, such as Lion Feuchtwanger and Emil Ludwig, and works of Thomas Mann (a Nobel Prize winner), Heinrich Mann, Arnold and Stephan Zweig and Arthur Schnitzler, and of Anglo-Saxon writers such as Upton Sinclair, Ernest Hemingway and Jack London. The destruction of books on sex by Dr Magnus Hirschfeld and other books classified as 'obscene' or 'trash' will cause no regret to the great majority of Germans. The burning began at 11.30. A dozen students, each carrying a book, were shepherded in turn by the Nazi organisers to the microphone, where each recited an appropriate couplet, ending with the words, 'I consign to the flames the writer Emil Ludwig,' or whoever the writer was. Then Dr Goebbels stepped into the glare of the searchlights and the bonfire, and declaimed

> against the 'filth' of the Jewish 'asphalt-literati'. In place of the literature destroyed a list of desirable books has been compiled and recommended to the public libraries, bookshops and general public. The list includes books extolling and explaining the principles of National Socialism, books on the theme of 'Nordic Racial Purity', and books romanticising war and explaining the virtues of a martial training.

Following the article, two additional stories were published, one concerning a 'Nazi threat to press in Bavaria' and another highlighting the publication of two pamphlets by the Jewish Communities of Great Britain titled 'Nazi Persecution of the Jews'. These articles exemplified, in a single page of a single publication, how the World's press were beginning to perceive events in Germany.

On 15 September 1935, a series of laws were enacted in Germany during a special session of the Reichstag, the German parliament, sitting in Nuremberg during the annual Nazi rally. These laws effectively stripped the Jewish people, along with any other non-Aryan sections of society, of all civil rights and citizenship. For those of us who enjoy the freedoms we exercise today, reading these pieces of legislation is shocking. The laws enacted were exceptionally draconian.

The original copies of the Nuremberg Laws are currently housed in the United States National Archives in Washington, DC.[5] These documents have been digitised and are accessible to the public through the US National Archives online collection. However, the documents' journey to the archives was eventful, ensuring sound provenance for those who questioned their authenticity.

In late April 1945, as the Third Reich disintegrated and Allied forces consolidated their positions within captured German

[5] United States National Archives, Collection PATTON, George S. https://catalog.archives.gov/id/18501106 accessed 11/5/2025

territory, United States Intelligence Corps Sergeant Martin Dannenberg was conducting intelligence operations in Bavaria. Following up on information received from an informant, he led his team to a bank vault in the town of Eichstaett, situated south of Nuremberg. There the sergeant acquired an envelope sealed with wax swastika stamps. Upon opening the envelope, he immediately recognised that he was holding a document signed by none other than Adolf Hitler. He summoned a colleague, Sergeant Frank Perls, to translate the documents. A Jewish German by birth, Perls had been baptised Protestant and had been compelled to flee Berlin in 1937. He had emigrated to the United States, where he joined the US Army in 1943 as an interpreter with the Intelligence Corps.

As Sergeant Perls read and translated the documents, Martin Dannenberg, looking on, observed that tears began to flow down his face. The magnitude of the discovery had profoundly affected his fellow sergeant, who realised that he was holding the original, signed documents that ultimately led to his family's persecution – the original Nuremberg Race Laws.

Sergeant Frank Perls recorded the circumstances of the document's discovery in a signed, typed statement dated 28 April 1945. This statement remained an integral part of the Nuremberg Laws file from that point forward.[6] It reads as follows:

> 1. Enclosed are two copies each of the three Nuernberg laws dated 15 September 1935 and signed by ADOLF HITLER and various other dignitaries. These are the original Nuernberg laws which were given as a special gift to the OBERBUERGERMEISTER Dr LIEBL by Hitler. At the approach of US troops the laws were given to the Hoehore SS and Polizei Fuehrer, General Der Waffen SS Benno Martin. This gentleman deposited

[6] Ibid.

these documents at the local Bank in BICHSTAETT where they were found today by the undersigned and Special Agent Martin Dannenberg of the 203rd CIC Detachment. Information as to the whereabouts of these documents were furnished by Herr Professor HANS RAUSCH, a high Official of the German FINANZMINISTERIUM and director of the Nurnberg office of the Finanzministerium (German Treasury).

A preliminary translation of the three laws is herewith attached.

The other letters in the enclosed envelope show only the manner in which they left the REICHSARCHIV and were sent to NUERNBERG.

Signed Frank R. Perls CIC

The documents were passed up the chain of command and were eventually entrusted to General George S. Patton, commander of the US Third Army. In violation of established protocols regarding the disposition of looted Nazi property, General Patton retained the documents and returned to California with them at the conclusion of the war. In June 1945 he deposited them with the Huntingdon Library in Los Angeles. Tragically, Patton passed away in a motor accident upon his return to Germany in December 1945, leaving no instructions regarding the original Nuremberg Laws. The documents remained undiscovered in the Huntingdon archive until 1999 when they were unearthed and subsequently lodged with the US National Archives in 2010. The two principal original laws, translated from German, outlined the following:

1. The Reich Citizenship Law *(Reichsbürgergesetz)* introduced legislation relating to the following:

Stripping of Citizenship: This law stated that only those of 'German or related blood' could be citizens of the Reich. Status as 'State Subjects': Jews were legally reduced to the status of 'subjects of the state', effectively stripping them of all political rights, including the right to vote or hold public office.

Racial Definition of 'Jew': A supplementary decree later defined who was considered a 'Jew' not based on religion, but on race (the number of Jewish grandparents), regardless of the individual's religious beliefs or practices.

2. The Law for the Protection of German Blood and German Honor (*Gesetz zum Schutze des Deutschen Blutes und der Deutschen Ehre)* likewise introduced further legislation covering the following subjects:

Prohibition of Marriage: This law strictly forbade marriages between 'Jews' and 'citizens of German or related blood'. Criminalisation of Sexual Relations: Sexual relations between Jews and non-Jewish Germans were also forbidden and labeled as *Rassenschande* ('race defilement').

Employment Restrictions: It prohibited Jews from employing female German citizens under the age of 45 in their households as domestic help.

Symbolic Restrictions: Jews were forbidden from flying the Reich or national flag or displaying the national colours.

These laws marked a dramatic escalation of anti-semitic legislation in Nazi Germany and served as a foundational legal step toward exclusion, segregation and, ultimately, the Holocaust. The racial definitions and restrictions of the Nuremberg Laws were later extended to other groups, such as the Roma (Gypsies) and Black people, defining them as 'alien to the Aryan species'.

The Nuremberg Laws were not formally enforced in Germany until after the 1936 Olympic Games had concluded to avoid drawing unwanted international attention that could have resulted in a boycott of the games, which were intended to showcase Nazi power. Following the conclusion of the games, German Jews effectively became Jews in Germany and, with the enforcement of the Nuremberg Laws and their subsequent amendments and additions, they were systematically robbed, segregated and, ultimately, exterminated.

The introduction of the laws also brought the means to enforce them. By 1938, this was carried out by the Gestapo, a secret police force ultimately under the command of Heinrich Himmler, who was appointed Reichsführer SS and Chief of the German Police in the Ministry of the Interior. The Gestapo operated independently of the civil and criminal courts and possessed extensive powers of arrest and detention that were administered outside of any court decisions or appeals. Their remit encompassed investigations into offences of treason, both high treason and state treason, sabotage against military targets and state or industrial infrastructure, and criminal attacks on the Nazi party and state. Additionally, the Gestapo's powers extended to the prevention of these offences through the use of surveillance and informants.

Himmler directed that the Gestapo be used essentially against people who 'by their behaviour endanger Volk and State', Volk meaning *volksgemeinschaft,* the ethnic community of the Aryan people; the Gestapo were to eliminate *Volksfeind* or 'the enemies of Volk', specifically communists, monarchists, political church groups – including Protestants and Catholics – homosexuals, freemasons and Jewry. In exercising these powers, a mere suspicion was deemed to be enough to form the reasonable grounds for arrest and detention. Detention without charge was referred to as *Schutzstaft* which translates, rather ironically, to 'protective custody', the Nazis' cynical euphemism for dangerous internment without trial. Initially, the duration of detention under protective custody was limited to three months. However, this restriction was subsequently lifted to permit unlimited periods of detention without judicial oversight. This period of detention was typically served in concentration camps.

The first concentration camp, Dachau, was established in March 1933, north-west of Munich. Conditions at Dachau were characterised by extreme brutality, including beatings, torture, starvation and disease. Over the years, the concentration camp system evolved with camps being constructed as sources of labour to support the Nazi war effort, for detention and, ultimately, for the extermination of individuals deemed enemies of the state.

Following the Anschluss, the Nazis swiftly imposed all the Nuremberg laws in Austria. Accompanying those laws was the enforcement by the Gestapo. Former Austrian police officials, many of whom were Austrian Nazis, who had previously been banned in Austria and had fled to Germany to avoid imprisonment, had been planning to seize control of the Austrian police system and establish their own for several years prior to March 1938. Franz Josef Huber, a head of the Gestapo in Austria, had been working in Germany's 'Austria' section of the Gestapo in Berlin since as early as 1933.[7] Huber and his team of senior officers swiftly assumed the role of policing in Austria.

From the night of 11/12 March 1938 a pogrom of terror was unleashed upon those known to be in opposition to the National Socialist regime. Lists had been compiled in Germany prior to the takeover which were subsequently augmented by those compiled by the Austrian National Socialists using their local knowledge and captured police files and suspect card indices. Immediately,

---

[7] *The Vienna Gestapo, 1938-1945 Crimes, Perpetrators, Victims*, Elisabeth Boeckl-Klamper, Thomas Mang, Wolfgang Neugebauer; Berghahn Books, New York, ISBN 978-1-80073-260-5.

blatant attacks were carried out on known Socialists, Communists and Nazi critics. Jewish homes and businesses were also targeted. On 16 March 1938 the entire police structure in Austria swore allegiance to Adolf Hitler.

Initially, the Gestapo established its headquarters in the ninth District at the Hotel Regina in Vienna following the formalisation of the Gestapo's structure and areas of responsibility being enacted in a decree issued by Reinhardt Heinrich on 18 March 1938. Subsequently, finding the Hotel Regina unsuitable, the Gestapo relocated its headquarters to the previously Jewish-owned and requisitioned Hotel Metropol at Morzinplaz 4 in the city centre on 1 April 1938.

During the initial six weeks of the annexation, mass arrests were conducted, resulting in an estimated 50,000 to 70,000 people, almost all men, being arrested. The Gestapo exercised its draconian powers and implemented its *protective custody* policy to persecute individuals deemed to be enemies of the state in Vienna. Many of those arrested were detained at the newly repurposed Hotel Metropol and released after a few days of interrogation. However, they were often re-arrested at a later date; others were subjected to extended periods of protective custody at Dachau Concentration Camp from which many did not return.

The name Dachau, which was unfamiliar before the Anschluss, quickly instilled fear among those who were at risk of persecution. Jewish business and shop owners who were detained and transported during the initial mass arrests often had 'holidaying in Dachau' painted across the frontage of their premises for those who remained to witness. While the initial days of occupation were marked by horrific events, the conditions for the Jewish people and other persecuted groups would deteriorate significantly.

Within a few weeks, in April 1938, Leopold discovered that the race laws applied to him. The fact that he had Jewish grandparents rendered him Jewish, regardless of his religious practice, as interpreted by the law.

On 1 April 1938 Gertrude recalled that her father left for work as usual but returned shortly after, well before his shift was due to end. Upon reporting to work, he was informed by his manager that, due to his Jewish ancestry, he was no longer eligible for state employment. Leopold was subsequently laid off, resulting in the loss of their primary source of income.

From that point on, Gertrude described her father as becoming quiet and reserved. He became reluctant to leave their apartment and frequently hid when he believed someone was approaching, fearing that the Gestapo had come for him.

Gertrude and Fritz continued their education at the school at Stromstrasse 78 as usual. However, shortly after the Anschluss, Gertrude noticed that the crucifix, which was typically displayed prominently in the classroom, had been removed and replaced with a photograph of Adolf Hitler. School life continued for the Kessler children under the Nazi regime until they were informed of the Nazi requirement that all children over the age of 10 were to join the *Hitlerjügend* or Hitler Youth movement. Gertrude vividly recalled coming home from school and enthusiastically describing the details of this new youth club to her parents.

> After Hitler came we were still at school. And we came home all excited. We were going to join the Hitler Youth, we were going to get uniforms. Up until then we had never heard the word 'Jew' in our house, Mum and Dad didn't ever use the word. I mean, Dad was just like any other Dad.

She expressed her excitement about the prospect of wearing a uniform, learning new skills, and participating in adventure activities outside of school. Leopold and Ernestine allowed the idea to linger in their children's minds for as long as it was safe before they had to explain the impossible to their children: that their father was Jewish which meant that, in the eyes of the Reich, they too were classified as *Mischlinge* or mixed race, but originally of Jewish blood. Consequently, this classification entailed various implications but, in the short term, it precluded their participation in the *Hitlerjügend.*

Gertrude later recalled how this perplexed her greatly. She had been raised as 'no religion', although she remembered that, around 1936, her parents had both her and her brother Fritz baptised as Christians in a Catholic Church. However, they never attended the church thereafter. Despite this, she was subsequently classified as a Jew and subjected to the full rigours of the Nazi racial laws. Leopold had undoubtedly anticipated the potential Nazi takeover as early as 1936 and had attempted to safeguard his family from the impending consequences.

A short time later, the Kessler children were compelled to relocate to a new school. Jewish children were no longer permitted to receive education in state schools; instead, they were mandated to attend an all-Jewish school in the 9th District at Währinger Strasse 43. This relocation from their original school in the 20th District necessitated a nearly 30-minute journey by foot and tram, as opposed to their previous 5-minute walk.

In June 1938 Gertrude Kessler concluded her term with two school reports, one from each of the schools she had attended that year. One report indicated that her school was located in 'Österreich' (Austria), while the other report stated that it was situated in 'Deutschland' (Germany). In an oral history recording describing the change, she remarked with a sense of almost childlike wonder,

> No more Austria. I was living in Vienna, Deutschland. Not Osterreich. That's after Hitler came. Fancy living in Deutschland? It was horrible! No more Vienna, Austria. Osterreich – and then it's Deutschland all of a sudden. I mean, people didn't believe it.

Observing the race laws' adverse impact on their children's lives, the Kesslers recognised the urgent need to remove themselves from the unfolding crisis. Initially, Leopold sought assistance from the Welfare Offices of the *Israelitische Kultusgemeinde Wien* (IKG), a Jewish community organisation headed by Viennese Jew Josef Löwenherz. Established in the early 1800s, the IKG served the interests of the Jewish community in Vienna. By 1938 it represented nearly 200,000 Orthodox Jews across Austria, all but 15,000 living in Vienna.

The IKG promptly received numerous requests for assistance with emigration, and the Gestapo actively encouraged and exploited these efforts to leave the country. But the Gestapo also raided the IKG's offices on 18 March 1938, seizing and examining all archived files and card indexes. This effectively gathered information on all Jewish individuals affiliated with the organisation.

In May 1938 the IKG was permitted to re-open under the supervision of the Gestapo and SA. It was renamed the 'Central Office for Jewish Emigration in Vienna', commonly referred to as the 'Central Office'.[8] Josef Löwenherz remained the leader of the Jewish community but, from that point, worked under the newly-appointed Director of Jewish Emigration in Vienna, SS Obersturmbannführer Adolf Eichmann, along with his second-in-command, Otto Kuchmann. Both Eichmann and Kuchmann were present during the 18 March raid. Consequently, the Nazis gained complete control over the eventual expulsion and deportation of the Jews from Austria. In the process, they used the existing Jewish IKG Council structure under Löwenherz to administer the process on their own people. This entailed enforcing and collecting a series of taxes and visa payments, including a 'Reich Flight Tax' designed to systematically rob every

---

[8] Yad Vashem, World Holocaust Remembrance Center; https://www.yadvashem.org/odot_pdf/Microsoft%20Word%20-%206394.pdf accessed 11/5/2025

Jew of practically their entire possessions prior to deportation. The original Jewish Council staff later found themselves compelled to work as 'researchers' and 'selectors', identifying the homes of the Jews that were to be raided, the occupants robbed and then deported. This was accomplished based on the information held in files and card indexes that the Jewish community had previously collected for welfare purposes.

To the IKG, Leopold Kessler initiated a first step in attempting to save his family. On 7 June 1938 he completed an application form purportedly designed to initiate his emigration process.[9] Upon reviewing the online copy of the original form today, one gains a sense of someone who, on the one hand, genuinely endeavoured to complete the form to the best of his ability, yet simultaneously recognised that his 'best' would never be satisfactory, akin to someone applying for a job with a CV that was far from adequate. It is evident from his responses that Leopold had reached a state of desperation.

The double-sided form was titled 'The Welfare Centre of the Jewish Community of Vienna Emigration Department'. The initial questions on the document were straightforward: name, address. In June 1938 Leopold's address was still given as 23 Leystrasse, stairwell 8, apartment 12, the *Red Vienna* apartment complex that Gertrude cherished. Leopold indicated his profession as a 'Goldsmith' with a specific specialisation of 'Ring maker', stating that he had trained as an apprentice until 1921 before transitioning to sales between 1921 and 1923 and subsequently being employed in a state abattoir from 1924 until April 1938. At that point, he declared his 'retirement', evading the fact that he had, in actual fact, lost his job due to racial persecution. He proceeded to provide details of his income at the time of application, which consisted of a monthly pension payment of 80 RM (Reichmarks). From this, he deducted 30RM

[9] Austria, Vienna, Jewish Emigrant Applications, 1938-1939; https://www.myheritage.com/research/record-11000-56397/leopold-kessler-in-austria-vienna-jewish-emigrant-applications

for 'interest' an 'electricity and gas', leaving a remainder of 50RM, which he wrote as '50RM for the living of 4 people!' The exclamation mark underscored the difficulty of making ends meet. To further emphasise this, in response to the subsequent question 'Are you able to obtain all the necessary documents for emigration?' he responded with a resounding 'No, if obtaining them would entail costs'. 50RM is roughly equivalent to £270 today.

On the reverse of the form, he indicated that his preferred destination was 'South or North America'. In response to the question 'What plans do you have for your new stay?' he replied, 'I intend to work as a labourer in any field (unskilled worker, etc.). My wife will seek employment as a janitor, waitress, etc.' He further stated that he had no means of emigrating, no relatives abroad in any of the countries he wished to emigrate to, and no passport. He included the details of Ernestine, Gertrude and Fritz on the form. When asked 'Which of the above-named relatives should emigrate now and which later?' he answered, 'If possible, all at the same time!' He again employed the use of an exclamation mark.

It has come to light that the completion of this form was a futile endeavour for Leopold, serving only to provide the Gestapo with intelligence on his family details, including his address and the anticipated amount of money they could extort from him in the months to come. Although the form was produced by the IKG, assistance from them was prioritised towards Jews affiliated with the Jewish *Kultusgemeinde* prior to the Anschluss, specifically Orthodox or 'full' Jews. However, the Nazi race laws defined Jews as anyone with Jewish ancestry, irrespective of their religious affiliation in 1938. In Austria at that time, this encompassed approximately 60,000 Catholics, 10,000 Protestants, and thousands more who adhered to no religion at all, including various groups such as socialists and freemasons, all now subject to persecution and subsequently attempting to secure escape routes from the country.

Other agencies were established in Vienna to provide assistance and potential emigration pathways based on religious affiliation.[10] The Catholic Church independently established a relief mission, with the Swedish Lutheran Church assisting Protestants. An independent operation was also initiated by a Dutch businessman named Frank van Gheel-Gildermeester, known as 'Aktion Gildermeester', to assist non-Orthodox Jews.[11]

The diverse sources of aid often resulted in individuals like Leopold traversing multiple organisations, spending extended periods in queues while enduring abuse on the street and, in some instances, physical violence. Those encounters were followed by the completion of paperwork at a cost, with the ultimate objective of obtaining an affidavit from a destination embassy to secure passage. Concurrently, the Nazi authorities continually revised regulations and amended their laws to ensure that applicants were returned to the initial stage of their process for even the slightest errors or deficiencies in completing the mandatory paperwork.

On 14 June 1938, one week after Leopold submitted his emigration application, Vice-Mayor Thomas Kozich of Vienna, who also held the position of head of the Nazi Party paramilitary wing, the *Sturm Abwehr* (SA), ordered the eviction of all Jewish tenants from State Municipal Housing. The effective date of the law's enactment was 31 July 1938. For many Viennese, covetous of Jewish families who had secured desirable housing in the relatively modern state housing apartment complexes, this was a signal to have them forcibly removed from their homes even before the enactment date. In various districts across the city, violence erupted and Jewish families were displaced from their homes and onto the streets with what belongings they could

---

[10] Raggam-Blesch, Michaela. ,Unexpected Alliances and Limits of Solidarity: Non-Jewish Aid Organisations and the Jewish Community Assisting Jews and 'Non-Aryans in Vienna, 1938–1945' Jewish Solidarity: The Ideal and the Reality in the Turmoil of the Shoah (2022).

[11] *Stemming The Dark Tide*, Shelia Spielhofer, Sessions of York, ISBN 1 85072 267 6

carry. At that time, Leopold's father, Salomon, still resided at 16 Hannovergasse in the 20th District, the original Kessler home. Salomon was forcibly evicted from the property and, at the age of 80, found accommodation in a hostel for elderly pensioners at Fugbachgasse 21 in Vienna's 2nd District, which was rapidly becoming a Jewish ghetto area within the city.

Salomon passed away ten months later on 21 May 1939, at the age of 81. The circumstances of his death remain unknown, but it is known that his remains were interred in an unmarked plot in the Old Jewish Cemetery at Simmeringer Hauptstrasse 234 in Vienna.

On 31 July 1938 the enactment of the Municipal Housing legislation compelled the Kessler family to vacate their apartment at Leystrasse 23. Subsequently, they secured rented accommodation in an apartment situated near Augarten Park at flat 41, 4 Streffleurgasse in the 20th District, on the boundary between the 20th and 2nd Districts. If Leopold's IKG emigration application, or any other application he may have submitted to an unknown organisation, was still pending, he would have been required to re-submit his paperwork, including the change of address, which would have further delayed the process. His situation was deteriorating rapidly.

Gertrude's recollection of her father standing outside this address with all the family belongings carried in a small handcart must have been a poignant snapshot of that moment. Leopold was emotionally devastated; he had lost his job, his home, his belonging, and had endured humiliation before his wife and children. He had been thwarted by the oppressive bureaucratic procedures designed to strip him of his possessions and, ultimately, eliminate him and his family. The modest apartment at Streffleurgasse was shared with other families who found themselves in similar circumstances. Over the ensuing months, their numbers would increase, all part of Adolf Eichmann's plan to confine groups of non-Aryans to designated locations in advance of the next phase of his evolving *final solution* to the Nazi Jewish problem.

From this juncture, Gertrude's recollections shifted to the more sombre aspects of the events that transpired around her. This suggests that during this period, she and her brother Fritz remained at home daily during their summer break from school. For instance, she was aware of the fact that their new apartment could not face the street. The rationale behind this restriction was that, during that era, individuals displayed Nazi swastika flags from their windows to express their support for the emerging regime. However, Jewish occupants were prohibited from displaying the Nazi emblem under the Nuremberg Race Laws and were instead mandated to display the Star of David from their property. This effectively marked their homes for attack and aided in the targeting of the occupants. The Streffleurgasse apartment faced the rear of the city block, not onto the main street. The registration document for the property was completed significantly by Ernestine, as Leopold, with his recently determined 'Nuremberg Law' Jewish background, was prohibited from doing so.

The Kesslers had carefully chosen their fourth-floor flat at the rear of the building, avoiding the dangerous obligation to display any dangerous symbol.

However, one aspect of the property location that Leopold and Ernestine could never have anticipated and which would haunt Gertrude for years to come was the street at Streffleurgasse where the apartment was situated. This street effectively formed one side of a rectangular block that bordered four- and five-storey buildings onto three other streets. Like much of the central districts in Vienna at that time, and still today, the upper floors contained housing apartments while the ground levels typically consisted of a mixture of business properties and housing. Streffleurgasse led onto Wasnergasse, which formed the boundary of the northern edge of the Augarten Park. Turning left and left again led into Unterbergergasse, from where a final left turn led into Karajangasse and back again to Streffleurgasse, completing the large rectangular city block. In the centre of the block, typical of the architectural layout of properties in Vienna, there was a large courtyard that could be overlooked from the Kesslers' fourth-floor apartment. In this instance, the courtyard formed within the four streets of buildings took the shape of the school playground for the Karajangasse Elementary School, which was accessed from Karajangasse. Today, a high school exists there called the Gymnasium Augarten, with a courtyard still in place as it was in 1938.

To Gertrude's horror, she discovered that the school overlooked by her apartment had been repurposed into a concentration camp. Following the initial wave of arrests of political opponents and Jewish individuals by the National Socialists, conventional prisons quickly reached full capacity. The Karajangasse school became the first in Vienna to be converted into an emergency detention centre, designed to hold prisoners until arrangements could be made to deport them by rail to the concentration camp at Dachau. Conditions in this new prison were brutal and provided a stark indication to those who could witness what transpired there of the potential consequences of National Socialist rule. An account survives from a man who was interned at the school during this period, a Jewish student named Erik Katz, who documented his experiences in writing after surviving the Holocaust.[12]

> Detainees were desperate. Hundreds of them were crammed into a classroom without desks. There was no place to sleep, no mattress, nothing. As it was a former school building, there were no bars on the windows. In desperation, some prisoners threw themselves from the windows of the upper floor into

---

[12] *Der Standard* 28 March 2024, https://www.derstandard.at/story/3000000211342/not-arrest-im-klassenzimmer-eine-schule-arbeitet-ihre-ns-geschichte-neu-auf

> the courtyard to commit suicide. The next morning, a policeman ordered every tenth prisoner to step forward. Then came his threatening voice: 'If one more of you Jews jumps from the windows to commit suicide, every tenth person will be shot. And anyone who comes near a window will get a bullet.'

Remarkably, Erik Katz's account, as a witness within the school, can be corroborated by that of Gertrude Kessler, who observed the events from outside and recounted them years later in her oral history interview.

> During the whole year we were there after Hitler did come we had to move from one house to another. Again we had front windows and you had to use the swastika flag and if you were Jewish you weren't allowed to put the flag out because those windows were known so we had to move to find accommodation where there were only windows at the back. The very first flat we found was looking into a concentration camp; a school taken over, and really, as children, we had to keep our blinds down. We had French blinds and we could sort of peep through them. I mean, it was dreadful to see Jewish people jumping out of fourth and fifth storey windows into the compound below to commit suicide. We saw all this going on from our back window.

Today, in the atrium, close to the entrance of the school, a memorial plaque displays the following information:

> Directly after the National Socialism annexation of Austria from March 1938 to 1939 thousands of opponents of National Socialism and Jews were

> captured by the Gestapo in this former elementary school. From there they were sent to concentration camps and many of them never returned. The surviving freedom fighters declared them 'Never to be forgotten' in 1945. That is why they always stand for an independent, democratic Austria.

It remains a haunting experience, armed with the knowledge of what transpired in the innocent surroundings of a primary school, to ascend the entrance steps and enter the same school courtyard, gazing upwards towards the rear windows of No. 4 Streffleurgasse. Contemplating the thoughts of the 15-year-old girl and her 13-year-old brother as they witnessed individuals driven to such a state of desperation that they resorted to suicide by jumping from the windows, one can only wonder how they could have ever comprehended the events unfolding around them. Did they ever question the extent of their parents' mental fortitude? If there was ever any indication to the Kesslers that they needed to take action to save themselves, this must have been it.

Ernestine assumed the primary responsibility of devising a means to rescue her family. Leopold, as a Jew, remained indoors to evade arrest for any infractions that could lead to his detention by the Gestapo or denunciation by neighbours, potentially resulting in his placement in *Protective Custody*. Ernestine, with her Catholic family background, retained the ability to pass herself off in public to conduct necessary inquiries and secure a way out of Austria. However, without valid passports, an offer of a visa and a substantial amount of hard cash, this objective was rapidly becoming unattainable.

As time progressed, the relentless introduction of legislation intensified the pressure faced by the Kesslers. On 31 May 1938 railway transportation of hundreds of arrestees commenced with their destination being the Dachau concentration camp. Subsequently, on 17 August 1938, all individuals deemed Jewish under the race laws, even those with non-recognisable Jewish names such as 'Kessler', were legally compelled to adopt the names *Israel* or *Sara*, respectively, for males and females. Leopold became Leopold Israel Kessler and Ernestine assumed the name Ernestine Sara Kessler from that date. Those names were to be used for all official documents and transactions, and their inclusion was to be announced with every introduction to prevent any confusion in social, business, or legal contexts. Failure to comply resulted in detention and transportation.

On 5 October 1938 a law was enacted in Germany that invalidated all passports belonging to Jewish individuals. If those passports were renewed, they were required to prominently display a large red letter 'J' stamp on the identification page, indicating that the holder was Jewish. This measure was a direct response to an appeal from immigration authorities in neighbouring countries, particularly Switzerland, who were experiencing a surge in Jewish tourists entering as visitors but failing to return.

Five weeks later, across 9 and 10 November 1938, a wave of violence erupted against Jewish populations across the entire Reich. Initially reported as spontaneous, this violence was, in fact, a consequence of a series of events that culminated in the assassination of a German diplomat, Ernst Vom Rath, who was stationed in Paris.

Two days prior, on 7 November 1938, a young Polish Jew named Herschel Grynszpan visited the German Embassy in Paris under the pretext of seeking assistance in addressing the deportation of his family, who were residing in Germany and were in need of refuge in a refugee camp located on the Polish-German border.[13] Ernst Vom Rath was assigned to handle Grynszpan's complaint within the embassy. When Vom Rath appeared before him, Grynszpan produced a concealed pistol and

[13] United States Holocaust Memorial Museum; https://encyclopedia.ushmm.org/content/en/photo/portrait-of-herschel-grynszpan accessed 11/5/2025

fatally shot him. Vom Rath succumbed to his injuries two days later and Grynszpan was swiftly arrested by the French police and handed over to the German authorities. Following his arrest he was executed but the specific date and location of his execution remain unclear.

Joseph Goebbels, the head of Nazi propaganda, swiftly exploited the incident to orchestrate a night of excessive violence against Jews throughout the Reich, deliberately portraying it as a series of spontaneous acts. However, the violence was far from spontaneous.

On the evening of 9 November, Goebbels, who was gathered with Nazi party members to commemorate the 1923 'Beerhall Putsch', issued an official directive prohibiting the Party from organising demonstrations. Nevertheless, he instructed, if demonstrations were to occur they were not to be obstructed.

The various assembled regional leaders mobilised their SA and Hitler Youth units, and violence, particularly directed against Jews, their business premises and Synagogues erupted in towns and cities across Germany and Austria. The night and the ensuing programme became known as *Kristallnacht*, aptly named due to the abundance of glass from broken windows of Jewish-owned properties that littered the streets for the days that followed.

Ironically, the German authorities asserted that the Jews themselves were responsible for the damage and violence that had transpired. Consequently, a one billion Reichsmark fine was imposed on the Jewish community and any insurance compensation claims for damage to Jewish-owned property, should they be made, were confiscated. A further series of anti-Jewish laws were subsequently introduced, severely restricting the lives of Jews. Those laws prohibited them from attending cinemas and theatres, revoked their right to hold driving licences and barred them from using public transportation.

Following those events, numerous arrests occurred. Notably, the arrests were solely based on ethnicity with individuals being arrested simply for being Jewish, rather than necessarily for violating any of the newly enacted laws and regulations. This aspect of *Kristallnacht* left a profound and lasting impression on Gertrude Kessler's young mind. She later recounted to her son, Charlie, the scenes of violence that erupted in front of her apartment on Streffleurgasse in Vienna. Additionally, she witnessed the repurposing of the Kajangasse School premises, which stood behind her apartment, into a detention facility for Jews awaiting transportation to the Dachau concentration camp.

The *Kristallnacht* pogrom and the horrific acts of violence witnessed by the Kesslers became a catalyst for action. As 1938 came to a violent end in Vienna, Ernestine Kessler discovered a potential solution. She learned that one organisation, established in the city since 1919 to assist the post Great War population during a period of near-famine, continued to maintain a presence after the Anschluss and remained committed to providing and co-ordinating aid across Austria to those in need. Gertrude, in an oral history recording made in June 1999, recalled the moment when her mother realised that assistance was available:

> My parents decided that this couldn't go on, that eventually we would end up in concentration camps … . They didn't know how to handle it because they didn't belong to anything, they didn't belong to the Orthodox Jewish religion, they didn't belong to anything Roman Catholic, they didn't belong to anything Protestant, they didn't belong to anything. One day my mother discovered that people called Quakers, the Society of Friends, were sending children like ourselves, children who had no-one to do anything for them. They said to my mother 'We'll try to get them out of this country'.

Although the Society of Friends provided a glimmer of hope, Ernestine and Leopold were confronted with an impossible choice that would have a profound impact on the lives and fortunes of their family, both in the immediate future and for years to come, with potentially positive and negative consequences.

CHAPTER 3

The Cardboard Suitcase

On an unknown date in early January 1939, Ernestine Kessler embarked on a journey to Singerstrasse 16 in Vienna's First District. Upon entering the imposing seventeenth-century Baroque-style Neupaurer-Brenner Palace building she traversed the grand entrance gateway. The magnificent facade, adorned with sculptures of the mythical Greek gods Hercules, Apollo, Flora and Hermes exuded a reassuringly solid presence. After navigating the throngs of desperate individuals outside, she found herself in a serene courtyard, an oasis of tranquility amidst the growing chaos of the city. This courtyard, and the offices surrounding it, served as the headquarters of The Society of Friends or Quakers in Vienna.

Since before the *Anschluss,* the Quakers had diligently provided assistance to those in need. In the subsequent months, their small team supported Non-Aryan individuals seeking to emigrate but who were unable to receive aid from other religious organisations such as the IKG, the Catholic Church or the Swedish Lutheran

Church, which primarily assisted those of Protestant faith. The Quakers also held a strategic advantage, having consistently refused to grant the Gestapo access to their records. They asserted that, as a neutral relief organisation, they transcended the Gestapo's categorisation of religious groups and societies in their new regulations.

On one occasion, two Gestapo officers attempted to gain access to the records at Singerstrasse 16 but were met with resolute refusal from the staff. The Gestapo surprisingly backed down and departed without further action.

From the summer of 1938 the IKG established the *Auswanderung von Jugendlichen*, a scheme for the emigration of minors. While the IKG primarily assisted its Jewish members, its welfare office collaborated with the Refugee Children's Movement (RCM) based at Bloomsbury House in London. The RCM effectively co-ordinated all child migration from Vienna and Berlin.

In November 1938, in response to the escalating perilous situation for Jewish families in Germany and Austria, the British Government granted permission for the unaccompanied emigration of children under the age of 17 from the Nazi territories. On 2 December 1938 the future Dutch resistance operative Geertruida Wijsmuller-Meijer, having gained knowledge of the desperate situation in Vienna, made a daring approach to Adolf Eichmann. In a heated head-to-head exchange, Wijsmuller-Meijer demanded that children be permitted to travel to Great Britain. Eichmann, seemingly unconcerned about the feasibility of the request, granted permission for 400 children to depart the following Saturday, the Shabbat. Knowing that this day was set aside by those of Jewish faith for rest and spiritual renewal, he likely recognised it as an unrealistic deadline.

Wijsmuller-Meijer promptly made the necessary arrangements with Bloomsbury House in London, the UK headquarters for the various organisations involved in the evacuation of child refugees. Notably, Bloomsbury House employed a Quaker office staff. The registration of children prepared to leave Vienna had already been completed by the IKG. Once trains were secured by Wijsmuller-Meijer, the transportation of the first 400 children became a tangible reality.

In fact, 459 child refugees departed Vienna on Saturday 10 December 1938. Fifty-nine of them disembarked in Holland, while the remaining 400 continued their journey to England where they were settled with the assistance of the RCM. By the end of December 1938 a total of 923 children had been evacuated from Vienna. From that point forward, a bureaucratic liaison was established at either end of the child refugee chain, establishing the *Kindertransport.*

Within the small courtyard at Singerstrasse 16, Ernestine was received and interviewed by Miss Brigit Kelsey, a Friends member responsible for children in Vienna. She was assisted at that time by her colleague, Franz Liposky, an Austrian native. The purpose of the interview was for Ernestine to register her two children, Gertrude and Fritz, for unaccompanied emigration to the United Kingdom. One can only imagine the intense conversations that Ernestine and her husband, Leopold, must have had in their small apartment at Streffleurgasse in the days following *Kristallnacht.*

The general situation in Vienna at that time was best described in an anonymous report prepared by a courier for the Nederlands Kinder Comité, the Dutch equivalent of the RCM.[14] In the report, the courier specifically mentioned meeting with 'Herr Lipopsky' of the Society of Friends at Singerstrasse 16 in Vienna. It also described the positions held by the other organisations attempting to evacuate children from the city and had a specific interest in the Dutch Aktion Gildemeester operations at the time.

[14] The Wiener Library, Report by a courier of the Dutch 'Kindercomité' regarding the situation in Vienna, https://www.pogromnovember1938.co.uk/viewer/!metadata/93912/1/LOG_0000/ accessed 11/5/2025

> Saturday morning 31 December 1938 [I] was sent to Vienna as courier of the Nederlands Kinder Comité. In accordance with my instructions I went to The Society of Friends, Singerstr. 16, for a meeting with Herr Lipopsky, in charge of the department for kindertransports to England and the Netherlands, who was not available, however.
>
> Then I visited Herr Gildemeester, for whom I had been given a message. He was not, however, inclined to discuss anything as he presumed the Gestapo would hear everything and that could have unpleasant consequences for him.
>
> Herr G. brought me to the Aktion-Gildemeester office, where I spent some hours and was told the following:
>
> It is as difficult for the emigration offices to get Jews over the German border as it is to get admission for them to another country. Each Jew means money for the German government, how they get it and by what means is immaterial to them. Even when all papers are in order, ticket paid, etc. the emigrants are sent back from the station and [they] try to get more money out of them … .

The courier further reported the following:

> The Gestapo had also been at the house of The Society of Friends and looked through all the books, which seemed not to indicate much, however, and they were left alone.
>
> It sometimes appears that the children who have transport opportunities and are on Herr L.'s list cannot be found any more. This happens because the families are often suddenly displaced from their house and then no longer have another fixed address.

This explains sending other children than those who are given to Herr L. by the Nederl. Comité.

Then Herr L. went with me to the Swedish Mission to take lists of Evang. [Evangelist] children who could possibly emigrate. In the waiting room there I saw various cases of frozen limbs as a result of spells in a concentration camp, incl. one young man whose hands remained thick and blue. He had already been in Dachau twice and was in danger of being arrested any time. Further variously crippled men (frozen feet) and one man with a totally bandaged head (frozen ears). Many cases occur particularly as the men are sometimes made to exercise day and night scantily clothed in a cotton jacket and trousers with a pair of shoes and bald shaven uncovered head. Whoever puts his hands in his pockets from the cold is struck with a club.

Herr L. told me afterwards that in a transport to the camp 200 men were loaded into a cattle truck and stood for 5 days and nights without food and water. Strong lights were brought onto the roof of this truck and the men had to look into the light without a break. Whoever bent his head was beaten to attention again. The truck was shot at if there was the slightest sound. The number reaching the camp no longer alive is not small. On arrival there they have to exercise for hours. If they complain of thirst, coffee is thrown on the stone floor which they can lick up.

In the race crimes section each man gets 5 kicks in the belly with a spiked shoe for each crime committed, many die here too. Another torture is to tie round the men's legs with a rope and in the room hoist them up to the ceiling with heads down, then the guards undo the rope. Many are smashed to pieces on the stone floor. This is a bloodbath each time. Men are laid on the floor in rows, they have to open their mouths wide and they urinate into their mouths. There are many indescribable variants of this policy.

As regards small things there is punishment of 20 lashes with a spiked stick, not administered by a single guard but by 20 different ones, so that each stroke is administered by a tireless arm. Each prisoner must sign a paper where only one small square is left blank for the signature; the rest is covered up so that no one knows what he is signing. They must also sign a piece of paper which says that they were never mistreated, had always eaten and drunk well, and they were forbidden to speak about their treatment in the concentration camp, on pain of death.

Machine guns are mounted at the four corners of the camp; anyone who goes outside after sunset is shot down without further ado. Prisoners may talk to each other for an hour a day; whoever says a word outside that time receives a number of blows. There is nothing to eat, drinking water is inadequate and polluted. There is also no heating, while the shelter is totally inadequate. There are men returned from Dachau who lost 30 pounds in one week.

Fatalities are reported to the family so they can come and fetch the urn; the body itself is never returned.

There is also a concentration camp for women guarded by men. One can imagine what this indicates. It seems not to be rare for Jewish girls of 12-14 years to be assaulted by SS or SA men. The emigration chances of these children are naturally extremely small, because one must wait for the results of this outrage. A few cases have nevertheless been transported to England.

All these stories were told to me by Herr Lipopsky, himself a full-blooded 'Aryan'.

The general misery in Vienna is unbelievable. There are people who have not had a roof over their heads for weeks, walking from doorway to doorway, who dare not report for emigration from fear of being arrested. Others, who no longer possess a cent, can get food at the K.G. to the value of 15 Pf. [Pfennig] per day.

From a statistic of one of the Jewish cemeteries in Vienna it appears that in the first weeks after 10 November 130 dead per day had to be buried. Many cemeteries were set on fire and the bodies lay open above the ground until the Jews themselves covered them with straw. The number of Jews killed on 10 November and later cannot be counted; they talk of hundreds.

The Dutch government has provided green cards for adult Jews, with which they are permitted to cross over the Dutch border with a valid passport. These cards are valid only three weeks. For those coming from Vienna, sometimes 4 to 5 days go by. As application for a pass without the possibility of emigration is pointless, and the minimum time required is three weeks, the cards expire before a pass is obtained. Nor can these cards be extended. In these ways emigration is made harder because a new application does not succeed. The cards should be valid for at least six weeks, as there is sometimes a delay through unpaid tax or fine.

In relation to the various offices in Vienna one has the strong feeling that Austria is treated harshly by the Netherlands, as the number of Austrian

> children in relation to the total number of emigrated children is particularly small, while the need in Austria is certainly no less.
>
> The motto of the Gestapo in Vienna is: 'The Jews shall not travel but perish.'

It is undeniable that, after reading the aforementioned report, which contains numerous references to Herr Lipopsky or 'Herr L' as he was referred to, Ernestine, if she had not already been aware of circumstances beyond her apartment and particularly within Dachau Camp, was left in no doubt by Franz Liposky and Brigit Kelsey that the only decision left to be made was to send her children to the United Kingdom. Given the escalating violence and the gradual but certain impoverishment, the Kesslers reached the conclusion that, with all available avenues of emigration as a family unit being denied to them, their prospects of survival were waning. However, there was this one opportunity to save their children. Ernestine and Leopold registered their children, Gertrude and Fritz, for unaccompanied emigration to a secure location outside of Austria.

The *Kindertransport* process typically took approximately three months to complete, from initial registration to final transportation. At each stage, the Quakers managed the applications and maintained communication with the IKG and the RCM at Bloomsbury House in London.

The process was not straightforward, and children were not automatically accepted for *Kindertransport.* Several stringent criteria had to be met before children's applications could be approved for travel.

Regrettably, the Kesslers' applications coincided with a significant surge in registrations for emigration. Many other families found themselves in similar or even more dire circumstances. During this period, the Kesslers still had a roof over their heads and were still a united family unit, although they were facing financial difficulties and were likely resorting to using any remaining savings to cover rent and food expenses.

The London RCM office mandated that all applicants provide certificates of health, both physical and mental, and also insisted that it could be demonstrated that all *Kinder* applicants had obtained a good level of educational attainment. Medical examinations were hastily obtained and Ernestine diligently gathered up the children's school reports, required to meet both the educational and mental health requirements imposed in order to showcase her children's potential 'social worth'.

If either the medical or the school reports were unsatisfactory, the application was declined, as the child was deemed unsuitable. Fortunately, in the case of the Kessler children, both sets of reports were exceptional.

One potentially problematic requirement imposed by London was an insistence on applicants providing four passport-sized photographs each.[15] Family or personal photographs were not acceptable. On the face of it, obtaining photographs should have been an easy task. However, for Jewish individuals or those deemed Jewish, no photographer in Vienna would engage with them. By this stage, Jewish photographic studios had either been closed down or their premises destroyed. The owners had either fled into hiding or been taken into detention. Additionally, Jews were prohibited from entering or conducting business in Aryan premises. Leopold Kessler resolved this by reaching out to an old family friend. Approximately fifty yards away, and just around the corner from both the original Kessler and Schrekinger family homes on Hannovergasse, was the photographic studio of Karl Piekarowitz.

Over the years, Karl Piekarowitz had photographed the Kessler family on various occasions at his Wallenstienstrasse studio. He had been in business since around 1915 and achieved

[15] Weindling, P. (2020). 'The Kindertransport from Vienna: the children who came and those left behind.' Jewish Historical Studies, 51(1). https://doi.org/10.14324/111.444.jhs.2020v51.003

success, leading him to expand and operate two studios in the 20th District of Vienna. By 1935, approaching his 60s, he had streamlined his business and operated from a single studio beneath his apartment at Rauscherstrasse 4, just north of the Augarten Park boundary in the city.

It is believed that Karl Piekarowitz set up his equipment at his Rauscherstrasse studio and discreetly photographed the Kessler children, providing the necessary passport-sized prints in accordance with the specified requirements. This undoubtedly expedited the process for the Kesslers and contributed to the successful completion of the documentation for the *Kindertransport* applications.

The photographs held significant importance for several reasons. Guarantors, individuals prepared to accept the children in the host country, received photographs to select prospective children. Cruelly, those photographs were also employed to ascertain any potential visible disabilities. Two photographs were retained in files in Vienna and London with the RCM. The remaining photograph was used to create an identity card, which replaced passports or visas for children entering the United Kingdom. The identity card issued to Gertrude containing her photograph remains with the family to this day.

The family's friendship with Karl and Helene Piekarowitz would later be put to the ultimate test and ultimately save Ernestine's life.

The final step in the process involved paying a guarantor's fee of £50 fr each prospective *Kinder.* In the case of the Kesslers, it appears that the Society of Friends covered this cost, as well as securing a willing guarantor.

As 1939 progressed, the *Kindertransport* trains continued to depart from Vienna, although none left carrying as many children as the initial December 1938 transport. Four further transports departed in the month of December, with the numbers on each reaching England being considerably fewer than the first train: 132 children, 68 children, 134 children and 117 children respectively. Consequently, for the month, the total number of children brought to safe locations within the United Kingdom was 923.[16] Then, in early January 1939, Josef Löwenherz was summoned to a meeting with Otto Kuchmann at the Central Office. The Gestapo media monitoring department had intercepted adverse reports in the British press following the arrival of the first *Kindertransport* at Harwich. Understandably, British journalists were intrigued by the story and several newspapers published photographs of a British policeman walking hand in hand with two young refugees at the dockside. The *Daily News* on 13 December 1938 carried a headline that read 'Children With Labels Meet The Man In Blue', while the *Daily Express* printed a similar story with the headline 'They came to England yesterday and found a friend directly they stepped off the boat – Children came from Vienna with 500 other refugees'. Other newspapers also carried the story with similar headlines, further drawing the British public's attention to the plight of Jews in Vienna and the specific circumstances faced by Viennese children. Kuchmann was incensed and threatened Löwenherz with the cancellation of all further transports should such stories appear again in the foreign press.

Meanwhile, the transports continued, and conditions became increasingly difficult for the Kessler family. In late March 1939, Ernestine and Leopold Kessler finally received notification that their children had been authorised for unaccompanied emigration via the*Kindertransport*. The date of travel was set for 26 April 1939 when Gertrude and Fritz were due to depart by train from Vienna's Westbahnhof railway station. Their final destination was determined as Londonderry in Northern Ireland.

Retrospectively, it is easy for us to accept that this was all an unfortunate event and that the children were saved, as if in some bizarre fairy tale. However, we must endeavour to understand the minds of Ernestine or Leopold Kessler or any of the hundreds of thousands of people across Europe at that time who

[16] Ibid.

faced impossible decisions. How could sending their children away, alone to a foreign land with an uncertain future, be considered a wise choice? In their minds, based on the unfolding horrors, did they dare to believe that they would ever see their children again?

Furthermore, once they made such a decision, how could they explain to a 13-year-old boy and a 15-year-old girl that the proposed course of action was the best option? To instil the necessary courage in all parties, Ernestine and Leopold must have recognised that their future in Vienna was bleak. They had run out of options.

We know that Franz Liposky at the Society of Friends was well-informed about the conditions at Dachau concentration camp. We can only assume that this information was passed on to the Kesslers, potentially serving as corroboration to what information they had gathered within their community or from the IKG or, for that matter, the scenes they had observed from the windows of their apartment.

As the departure date of 26 April approached Ernestine encountered a daunting challenge: what could she send with her two children who were essentially leaving her forever? This was particularly difficult considering her limited resources and the need to create an optimistic outlook for them, regardless of the uncertain future that lay ahead. She had to ensure that they believed in the possibility of re-uniting with their parents.

Stringent regulations regarding the Kindertransport applied to this aspect but Ernestine, understandably, deviated from those regulations to provide a better future for her children. Each child was permitted to carry one suitcase. Charlie, for instance, recalled that his mother had brought a small suitcase from Vienna, approximately the size of a leather school satchel; he had often seen it as he was growing up. However, it was not made of leather but rather of a heavy cardboard-like material coated with shellac or varnish for added strength.

Several items that are still in the family today originated from Vienna in 1939 and were carried by Gertrude in the small suitcase. These included her school reports which had facilitated her successful application for the IKG Kindertransport. For Ernestine, those reports were crucial in forming the basis of a sound curriculum vitae for her daughter.

Clean clothes that would last for two weeks were packed in the suitcase, along with photographs of Ernestine, her parents and Gertrude. Ernestine had prepared bread and biscuits using all of her rationed supplies and packed them in the suitcase for the journey. Gertrude also packed a small blue ceramic flute of a peculiar design known as an Ocarina. A scarf, knitted with decorative bobbles was also included and later became a treasured lifelong possession.

Taking a calculated risk, Ernestine concealed a number of gold twenty-five schilling coins in the children's clothing. The coins belonged to the family and constituted a large part of their remaining resources, primarily used for bartering. At that time, they were no longer legal tender in the *Ostmark,* as Austria had been renamed, but held value due to their gold content, similar to United Kingdom gold sovereigns. The precise number of the coins owned by the family is unknown. However, several coins remained in the family's possession in Northern Ireland until the 1970s. Neither Gertrude nor Fritz were ever compelled to exchange them for cash. It is believed that Leopold acquired them from the remnants of his father's gold and jewellery business. They were certainly not disclosed to the IKG and were most likely concealed within Gertrude and Fritz's clothing for the duration of the journey.

One of Gertrude's notable possessions was a little notebook, measuring approximately six inches by four inches in size and of modest thickness. Bound in deep-red leather, it contained approximately fifty pages. On the front cover, Ernestine had affixed a small label and, in her own German handwriting, she had inscribed the title *Deutsches Kochbuch*, or German Cookbook.

The interior of the notebook was meticulously filled with every cooking and baking recipe that Ernestine possessed, accompanied by the corresponding ingredients, weights and cooking instructions. This small volume encapsulated the knowledge that Ernestine intended to impart to her daughter over the years, condensed into a single tangible resource as their lives were about to be torn apart.

Regrettably, Gertrude was denied the intimate secrets of life that a mother shares with her daughter to prepare her for the challenges of adulthood. In the ensuing years Gertrude cherished and diligently used the book to its fullest potential, preparing the European delicacies that later distinguished her family's cooking from their County Fermanagh neighbours.

The final pages of the notebook contained invaluable information that would serve Gertrude during her journey. These entries diverged from the cooking recipes in that they were written in Gertrude's own handwriting, not that of her mother. The details were meticulously crafted to ensure their confidentiality, comprising a list of names and addresses of contacts, provided to her by the Society of Friends in Vienna, who could be contacted for assistance in the event of difficulties during the *Kindertransport* process. To protect the identities of those individuals, Gertrude had strategically written the names and addresses across six pages in the book.

Upon reaching a secure location, Gertrude could effortlessly access the information by carefully removing the middle two pages of the section, revealing the original first and sixth pages that could be read across both remaining sides. The book continues to be cherished by the family today and, when examined, the two middle pages, having been removed, allows the complete list of details to be read easily. For instance, the first entry on the left side of the first of the six-page section reads: 'Society of Friends Miss Kel.' Six pages later, the entry continues: 'Sey 1 Singerstr. 16', with the complete entry reading 'Society of Friends Miss Kelsey 1 Singerstr. 16'.

Clearly, this level of encryption would not have posed any significant challenge for the Gestapo code-breakers to decipher. However, it demonstrates Ernestine's meticulousness and caution in preparing her children for their perilous journey. The manner of her writing may just about have perplexed a German border guard with limited English language proficiency. The entry also reveals her determination to protect their helpers in the event of Gertrude's luggage being searched during her dangerous journey.

Without a doubt, Miss Kelsey was a lady deserving of protection. Her name, recorded in the small cookbook, indicates that she served as the primary contact for the Kessler family within the Society of Friends at Singerstrasse 16. Furthermore, details from a Quaker German Emergency Committee staff list dated March 1939 reveal that the 'Miss Kelsey' mentioned in Gertrude's notes was indeed Brigit Louise Kelsey. Within the organisation of the Vienna Friends, Brigit is recorded as having held the specific responsibility for 'Children'.

On the United Kingdom opening its borders to the *Kindertransport,* Brigit assumed the role of interviewing, assessing and processing the applications of approximately 3,000 *Kindertransportees* who sought refuge from Austria in Vienna and presented themselves at Singerstrasse seeking assistance. Brigit was well aware of the perilous circumstances faced by those desperate individuals. At first hand she witnessed the crowds of persecuted Non-Aryans lined up outside, subjected to taunts, abuse and assaults from the passing Nazi population.

Brigit was aided in this endeavour by Franz Liposky who provided translation assistance during the interview process, along with another Quaker working in Vienna, David Hodgkin. Those who eventually made their way from the chaotic scene outside Singerstrasse 16 to the orderly calm within, to be eventually introduced to Brigit Kelsey, found themselves in the hands of an individual uniquely qualified to alleviate their fears and concerns. Brigit was a resolute individual who possessed the determination and organisational skills to safeguard them from harm.

[17]At the age of 30 Brigit Kelsey possessed an unassuming and amiable demeanour. She wore round-rimmed spectacles, which were fashionable during that era, and had a slender build but a strong character. Brigit was born in Burnham-on-Sea, Somerset, England, as the only child of her parents. Tragically, when she was just 3 years old, her father was killed while leading an expedition in Africa. The expedition involved attempting to drive from Cape Town to Cairo by car. Brigit received her education at a boarding school which her mother was only just able to afford after her father's death. On leaving school she was inspired by and befriended the Belgian politician Lucie Dejardin who encouraged her to study social work. At the age of 18, her mother passed away, following which she overcame this further tragedy and found the strength to move to London alone to pursue her studies in social work. She obtained a diploma in the subject from the London School of Economics with which she secured employment with London County Council where she played a key role in establishing childcare programs in the inner-city areas.

At this juncture Brigit developed a profound passion and love for adventurous travel. She embarked on numerous expeditions, including treks in the Alps and a remarkable canoe journey from Regensburg in Germany, down the River Danube to Vienna, a river trip of approximately 100 miles. Her experiences in those challenging environments undoubtedly equipped her with the confidence and resilience to address effectively the concerns of children and parents seeking her assistance. Brigit possessed the ability to navigate stressful situations independently, having previously transformed her own misfortunes into positive actions.

In Vienna, from late 1938 to 1939, Brigit used her skills to provide a means of escape for the countless families in dire need of assistance. The Society of Friends' operation in Vienna was

[17] Information provided to the author from the Hodgkin family, Australia 2025.

relatively understaffed in comparison to the overwhelming volume of individuals who sought help at Singerstrasse. The Vienna International Centre, as it was known, operated with a core staff of approximately eight or nine individuals, whose numbers fluctuated due to staff appointments, from the UK and the USA. During the 1938 and 1939 periods the senior members of the Centre consisted of Emma Cadbury and Ethel Haughton, supported by a smaller team of Austrian administrative assistants and typists.[18]

As the political situation in Vienna deteriorated following the *Anschluss*, the role of the Centre underwent significant changes. The threat of Nazi religious persecution led to a decline in the attendance of local individuals at various Quaker study groups and meetings. Consequently, the local staff numbers dwindled as it became increasingly hazardous for many of them, particularly those of Jewish descent, to report regularly to Singerstrasse for employment as it was believed that the premises were under surveillance by the Gestapo. As the workload of the Quaker Germany Emergency Committee increased, the frequency of regular meetings and activities decreased until eventually assistance for those being persecuted became the primary focus of the Centre's efforts.

A subsequent entry in Gertrude's Cookbook underscores how the Friends at Singerstrasse 16 successfully relocated and adapted to the evolving circumstances while maintaining their *Kindertransport* responsibilities. The entry, written under the same clandestine security measures as 'Miss Kelsey', reads 'Miss Merry Campbell', then, six pages later, continues 'Bloomsbury House London WC1'.

'Merry' was, naturally, Gertrude's phonetic rendition of Mary Campbell's name. Mary Campbell was an English Quaker who had worked at Singerstrasse in Vienna until the summer of 1938. She had actively participated in organising the Vienna component

---

[18] *Stemming The Dark Tide*, Sheila Spielhofer, Sessions of York, ISBN 1 85072 267 6

of the *Kindertransports* before relocating to London. It remains uncertain whether she encountered any perceived threats that compelled her to leave Vienna at that time. On her return to London, she assisted in staffing the Quaker liaison offices at the RCM in Bloomsbury House. Her unique knowledge of both sides of the evacuation process undoubtedly assisted decision-makers in London in comprehending the frustrations and difficulties experienced by the Friends in Vienna. Upon establishing herself in London, Mary Campbell became the primary point of contact for the Kessler children on their arrival in England.

Accounts preserved today, written by former *Kindertransport* evacuees, provide a vivid portrayal of the children's journey. A documentary film produced in 2000 by Deborah Oppenheimer, titled *Into The Arms of Strangers*, described the experiences of several men and women who were evacuated to England in late 1938 and 1939 as children. Those accounts offer valuable insights into the apprehensions and concerns of the children, as well as the conditions they endured during their journey to safety. In a rare interview, Lore Segal, a child evacuated from Vienna, told how her parents insisted she go:

> My father said, 'Mummy and I cannot leave but you are going to leave' I said what do you mean I'm going to leave, wait a moment. He said, 'You're going to England', when? 'Thursday,' he said.

Lore's mother, Franzi Groszmann, a survivor of the Shoah, described the pain of the separation:

> I knew that I ought to want to send her away but I couldn't imagine to give her permission to go. My husband said 'she must go' and he didn't listen to me, he just arranged everything for her and I had to give in and I saw in the end that he was right. But the hurt is unbelievable, that cannot be described.

Hedy Epstein, who was evacuated from Germany on a separate *Kindertransport* train, recalled the moment of departure in a similar way to Gertrude Kessler as she watched as her mother ran along the station platform:

> My parents ran along with the train on the platform and I still remember in my head I heard that refrain 'you're leaving, you're leaving, you're leaving' and I watched their faces and tears were streaming down their faces, down their cheeks and I knew then that these people really, really loved me. This is why they are sending me away.

Ursula Rosenfeld remembered approaching the Dutch border on the first day of the journey. The train stopped at the last station before the frontier and the Nazi border guards boarded the train:

> The Nazi border guards, very officiously came round and made some of the children open their suitcases. They shouted at us and threw their weight about.

Alexander Gordon, another refugee, also recalled passing through the border:

> They were looking for new things, new clothes and they didn't like that. They gave the children a tough time, several were crying, and we were there quite some time and they enjoyed doing what they were doing to us. Then suddenly we were in Holland and we were free.

Ernestine Kessler's decision to conceal valuables within her children's belongings appears to have been a calculated risk that proved successful, considering the potential repercussions of such valuables being discovered.

In the Netherlands, the train transported the children to a seaport where Gertrude and Fritz boarded a ferry that carried them to the English port of Harwich. Gertrude was unaware that she had actually boarded a ship; she had merely followed the group of other *Kindertransport* children through a large hall at the quayside. From Harwich, another railway journey brought them to Liverpool Street Station in London. There, fostering parents and RCM officials verified their information against data the waiting children had brought with them. Ultimately, all the children were matched with their sponsor family members or agency staff and departed the station to commence new lives. Gertrude encountered numerous bureaucratic obstacles in securing their emigration visa documents. In her later years, she vividly recalled desperately seeking offices and officials in London, despite her inability to read or speak English. After an arduous wait, they discovered that their journey had not yet reached its destination. Eventually, it was explained to them that their intended destination was 'Londonderry, Ireland'. Prior to this revelation, Gertrude had been unaware that they had two seas to cross. She summarised her experience of this part of the journey:

> In London they put us on a train and I remember having a card hanging here [around her neck] saying 'Gertrude Kessler' and my brother had one 'Fritz Kessler' and we were going to Ireland … we didn't eat, we didn't drink, we didn't do anything, we just wept, my brother was just thirteen and a half and I was just fifteen.

Finally, on Saturday 29 April 1939, after another ferry journey the two children arrived at the port of Belfast in Northern Ireland, having travelled for a total of three days and three nights. On their arrival in Belfast, they were met by a Quaker representative of the German Refugee Committee. The representative's identity remains unknown, but it is possible that it was one of the individuals whose Belfast addresses were listed in the Cookbook. This representative, who was fluent in German, informed Gertrude and Fritz that they were being taken to Derry, where a family was prepared to provide them with shelter. Subsequently, the lady placed them in a car and drove them to a location just outside the city where they were shown their new residence and introduced to their new family. On their first night in Northern Ireland however, things did not go as planned.

The vehicle that transported the children to Derry drove into the surrounding countryside where it came to a halt at the residence of a local family who had consented to host the children as part of the *Kindertransport* initiative. Gertrude and Fritz were introduced to their newfound family and offered a meal, which Gertrude later described as 'just rhubarb'. She had never encountered this culinary delicacy before and promptly instructed Fritz to refrain from consuming it. They were then led to their bedroom and shown their beds which were constructed entirely of straw. For Gertrude, this revelation proved to be the final straw, prompting her to make a swift decision to leave immediately:

> Coming out from Vienna, a very modern city, we had beds at home and a bathroom and we had toilets, they had nothing … . We decided, the next morning that we weren't staying there, so we disappeared. We took our little case that we had with the food that had gone blue mould inside because we couldn't eat. Anyhow, the next morning we took the little case and we walked down the road from the farmhouse, we

> couldn't say we were going, we couldn't speak! So we walked right down to the river at Londonderry and we walked on, it was a long way. We got to the bridge and we thought we could get a boat there back to Vienna. All we wanted was to go back home. We couldn't care about Hitler or anything, just home. We just missed our parents and missed home.

At Craigavon Bridge in Londonderry, two young refugees stood contemplating their next steps. Remarkably, a car pulled up beside them, its driver being none other than Mr Friedrich, or Fred Szilagy; his name was inscribed in the Cookbook as 'Szilagyi'. The address provided in the book was 9 Strand Road in Londonderry. Fred had been informed that the Kessler children would be arriving in Londonderry and was en route to check on their well-being when he noticed two individuals who appeared to be refugees standing at the bridge.

Fritz Kessler, dressed in traditional Austrian *Lederhosen* trousers, and Gertrude, wearing knee-high socks, were easily identifiable as refugees. Fred invited them into his car and drove them back into the hills and the host farm. After providing necessary explanations, he put them up in his own home, a small flat on Strand Road in the city, for a few nights before transferring them to the Childhaven Orphanage in the seaside village of Millisle, County Down.

Fred Szilagy was aware of the plight of the young Kesslers. In fact, he and his family had fled Vienna the previous year at the time of the Anschluss and settled in Londonderry. He was acquainted with Leopold Kessler, having worked with him in Vienna, which suggests that the inclusion of his name in the Cookbook was not a coincidence. He was likely familiar with the family and was on his way to visit the new arrivals when he noticed them on the side of the road.

From this point forward, with regard to the Kessler children, the Belfast Committee for German Refugees assumed primary responsibility for their care. The Committee, headquartered at the Methodist Church's Grosvenor Hall in Glengall Street, Belfast, co-ordinated representatives from various religious denominations in providing assistance to refugees seeking escape from Nazi-occupied Europe at that time.[19] Through their dedicated efforts, the various church groups secured placements for both employment and educational opportunities as well as suitable accommodation for refugees of all ages arriving in Northern Ireland. The Kesslers were among many who greatly benefitted from the support networks of the Society of Friends.

The Kessler children settled into their new lives at the Childhaven orphanage in Millisle. They enrolled in the local school and found themselves surrounded by other refugee children whose parents had also made the impossible decision to send their children to safety. Gertrude and Fritz blended in with other children of various ages from Vienna who arrived in Millisle until the end of September 1939, the month that war broke out and the *Kindertransports* ceased.

Among the Millisle *Kinder* were *f* Nussbaum, Pauline Spitz, Erna Sojfer, Henry Hirsch and, unrelated to Henry, from the German city of Dresden, Walter Hirsch.[20] They didn't know then, and for the rest of their lives, that their parents would join others in a Nazi-occupied school in Vienna and a train which would take almost all of them to their deaths in Poland.

[19] Friends' School Archive material, Friends' School, Lisburn, Northern Ireland.

[20] Millisle Primary School archives, Millisle, County Down, Northern Ireland.

CHAPTER 4

Transport Number 4

On 1 September 1939 Nazi Germany invaded Poland. Two days later, Britain and France declared war on Germany after Hitler ignored their ultimatum to withdraw from Poland. Sixteen days later, following a pact agreed between Germany and the USSR, the Red Army invaded Poland from the east. Consequently, Poland was divided, with the regions under the control of both armies annexed and placed under the dominions respectively of Nazi Germany and the USSR. The Germans renamed the area of central Poland under their control the *Generalgouvernement* or General Government region. The *Generalgouvernement* was placed under the administrative charge of Hitler's cabinet member and personal lawyer Hans Frank who held the formal title of Governor General of the occupied Polish territories. The original Polish population of the area was deemed stateless by the Nazis and the region was administered entirely by Nazi officials with none of the original Polish government structure retained. Notably, the name 'Poland' was no longer to be used in Nazi terminology.

The outbreak of the Second World War marked a turning point in the lives of Ernestine and Leopold Kessler in Vienna. The *Kindertransports* came to an end as borders closed and efforts to evacuate the thousands of persecuted adults and their children were suspended as the various co-operating embassies closed their doors, making the provision of affidavits, the documents essential for emigration, impossible. Non-German or Austrian staff members assisting those in need were compelled to leave the country as they were from that point classified as enemy aliens. This development had a significant impact on the activities of the Society of Friends. One week prior to the invasion of Poland the Society's office in Vienna had received a secret communication urging it to relocate all non-Austrian staff members to Switzerland on a 'temporary vacation'.[21] The society took this advice seriously and relocated, leaving only three staff members, Käthe Neumayer, Grete Sumpf and Franz Lipovsky, along with their front door receptionist, Konrad Schillinger, to provide what aid they could to those thousands of people still in need.

The seismic historical and political events that erupted across Europe in the ensuing months brought together a small group of individuals who found themselves unexpectedly connected by a train journey from Vienna. Despite having no prior common ground, this group shared a common bond: a determination to survive for the sake of their children and, in the case of single adults, themselves.

***

Paul Messinger was born into a Jewish family on 25 May 1914 in Krakow, Poland. The son of Leopold and Jetty Messinger, Paul was raised in Krakow, although he and his family held

[21] *Stemming The Dark Tide*, Sheila Spielhofer, Sessions of York, ISBN 1 85072 267 6

Austrian citizenship. Paul had a younger brother, Heinrich, born in 1915, shortly before the death of his father, following which his mother remarried and had a daughter named Elisabeth to her second husband, Alfred Vermes. Elisabeth Vermes was born in 1929. Shortly thereafter, the family relocated to Vienna, where they lived at Neustiftgasse 93 in the 7th District. Both Paul and his brother Heinrich enrolled in the University of Vienna in 1933 and 1934 respectively, both pursuing studies in Medicine.[22]

Shortly after starting his studies, amidst the socialist opposition to the prevailing *Austrofascism,* Paul joined the *Rotes Studenten Verein* Red Students Association (RSV), an illegal organisation formed by communists and revolutionary socialists. Operating within the University of Vienna, the RSV was led at that time by Viennese chemistry student Hans Friedmann, known to other RSV members by the pseudonym 'Egon'.[23]

The group operated in secrecy, employing a cell structure whereby small groups of five members formed a 'cell' of activists. Only one member in each cell was privy to the identity and codename of their counterpart in another cell, ensuring minimal disruption in the event of arrests. The limited knowledge among members diminished the potential impact on the organisation in the event of action taken by the authorities. The RSV engaged in various anti-fascist propaganda operations on the university campus and the surrounding area, consistently highlighting resistance against the Dolfuss regime. Their operations included the covert distribution of leaflets and pamphlets, the raising of flags within the complex and the painting of slogans. Following the *Anschluss* and Nazi occupation in 1938, the RSV continued to operate, albeit under heightened risks. Their activities were subsequently classified as treason and investigations into their

[22] Messinger Family Archive material, David Messinger, Haifa, Israel.
[23] Memorial Book for the Victims of National Socialism at the University of Vienna, https://gedenkbuch.univie.ac.at/en/person/hans-friedmann accessed 11/5/2025.

activities and membership became subject to the jurisdiction of the Nazi Gestapo.

Paul soon fell foul of the Nazi regime. It banned Jews from universities as students or lecturers. Furthermore, Jewish administrative staff were prohibited from working in university premises. The most devastating directive was the declaration that the academic qualifications of Jewish students were deemed invalid. Consequently, after years of study, Paul Messinger, his brother Heinrich and over 2,700 others connected with the University of Vienna were forced to cease their studies and leave the university. Paul had been completing his final year of his medical degree and was close to qualifying as a doctor.

Despite the escalating persecution and violence, Paul continued to resist the regime in any way possible.[24][25] He volunteered to assist the Operation Gildemeester organisation in Vienna, which was involved in aiding individuals seeking to emigrate. During his time there, he discovered that Adolf Eichmann and the Gestapo had infiltrated the organisation and intended to exploit the information held on those who had applied to emigrate for their own forced deportations. Paul set about altering the documents held and, to a certain extent, thwarted several of the intended Nazi deportations. However, his actions had significant repercussions for his own future. In August 1938, Paul's brother Heinrich acquired an emigration visa to Uruguay through Operation Gildemeester. He managed to make his way to Portugal and, from there, embarked on a ship to Montevideo where he eventually settled. The remaining Messinger family members were unfortunately unable to secure their escape and were forced to stay in Vienna.

In June 1940, following a Gestapo search of the Operation Gildemeester offices, Paul was arrested. He had just married his

[24] Messinger Family Archive material, David Messinger, Haifa, Israel.
[25] Leo Baeck Institute Archives; Messinger, Heinrich. [Biographical notes on Heinrich and Paul Messinger] / Heinrich Messinger. (1995).

wife Erna two weeks previously.[26] Paul was questioned about the altering of the files about those who had originally registered for emigration but whom Eichmann and the Central Office intended to transport to the newly renamed *Generalgouvernement* region of occupied Poland. Paul, solely responsible for the alterations, could not deny the allegations against him. He was found guilty of sabotage by the Gestapo and sentenced to transportation to a labour camp in Mitterweissenbach, in Upper Austria. His time there was arduous from the beginning; he had been marked with a red dot beside his name on the transportation list, indicating his socialist inclinations and making him a target for more severe treatment. After approximately three months of detention, he was released and returned to his wife Erna and their home at Neustiftgasse in Vienna's 7th District.

***

Helene König was born in 1890 and raised in Berlin.[27] She was the daughter of Jewish parents, Philipp and Perle, or Paula Anstreicher, who had originally emigrated from the western Ukrainian city of Lviv. During that era, Lviv was also known as Lwów and also Lemberg, depending on the period of Polish, Russian or German rule. Helene settled in Berlin where she married her husband Jakob and established a successful fabric wholesale business. In 1926 she had a daughter named Felicitas. Helene continued to operate her business successfully until Adolf Hitler came to power in Germany in 1933. From that point on, the family became victims of the Nazi anti-Semitic Nuremberg laws. Following an incident at her business, Helene was denounced by a disgruntled employee who happened to be friendly with an SS officer. Consequently, the family was forced to flee for their safety to Prague, in what was then known as

[26] Ibid.
[27] The Wiener Library, File 02/239, Helene König-Rösler: Experiences of a Jewish lady in Czechoslovakia-Austria and Poland.

Czechoslovakia, where they stayed with relatives. They initially relied on their savings but, by 1936, Helene's financial resources were dwindling and she was forced to take decisive action to rebuild her business and secure an income for her family. Taking advantage of the fact that she held an Austrian passport, she made a courageous decision to relocate to Vienna alone, leaving her husband Jakob with their daughter in Prague. Her objective was to establish a textile wholesale business in Vienna and hopefully prepare the way to bring her family to join her once she had achieved some financial stability.

Initially, Helene's endeavours paid off. By January 1938 she had established the new business and started trading, harbouring the hope of re-uniting with her husband and daughter. Within a mere three months, however, all was lost. With the arrival of the Nazis in Austria in March 1938 and the ruthless, swift implementation of the Nuremberg Laws, the same laws which had forced her out of Berlin, her business was forcibly seized from her. Helene tried in vain to return to Prague to be with her young family but her attempts were repeatedly thwarted by the stringent regulations imposed at Austria's frontier.[28] Amidst desperate circumstances, she liquidated her business assets and sought temporary shelter by working at the Jewish old people's home on Seegasse 9 in Vienna's 9th District. This separation from her daughter and husband exacerbated her anxieties. As the weeks passed, the residence at Seegasse 9 experienced a rapid influx of homeless Jewish elderly residents who had lost their homes to Aryanization or were left without caregivers due to the deportation or detention of their family members. From mid-1939, elderly Jewish individuals were also barred from residing in non-Jewish old people's homes and were forced to find accommodation elsewhere. The Seegasse 9 residence, at that time the largest in Vienna, quickly became overcrowded due to the increasing number of residents and the decreasing number of care staff. The impact of food rationing, which was implemented

[28] Ibid.

upon the declaration of war, further exacerbated the situation, transforming the home into what essentially became a concentration camp for the elderly.

***

In May 1939 a *Kindertransport* train brought 10-year-old Anna Nussbaum, along with eighty-three other children from Vienna to Harwich and then on to London. There she waited anxiously and alone while all her travel companions were collected by their sponsoring adults until she was finally told that she had to travel further, again alone, to Northern Ireland. She arrived at Millisle in County Down on 20 May and settled in with the other refugees and locals at the Millisle school, quickly making many new friends.[29] She encouraged her new friends to write messages and sometimes contact details in a little notebook which she had brought with her from Vienna and into which her father, Schaje, had made the first entry in Vienna on 9 January 1939 when he wrote 'Flowers wither, but the faithful love of the heart remains forever green'.[30]

In Vienna Anna had lived at the family apartment at Wehlistrasse 20 in the second district along with her mother Rebekka and older sister, Klara. In late 1938 Klara was evacuated to Dublin as part of an earlier *Kindertransport* train while Schaje and Rebekka waited for a response to their own IKG emigration application which was applied for when the family were still all together in May 1938.

---

[29] Millisle Primary School archives, Millisle, County Down, Northern Ireland.

[30] Memoir book of Anna Nussbaum, later Chana Gross, born in Vienna, Austria in 1929, with inscriptions by her girlfriends in Vienna, Belfast and Millisle, Ireland and in London during 09/01/1939-17/07/1947; and her memoirs, Yad Vashem Archive, https://collections.yadvashem.org/en/documents/13417501 viewed 11/5/2025

From early September 1939 events transpired that would have serious repercussions for the Jewish population across Europe. The German and Soviet invasions of Poland and the subsequent partition of the country between the two invading powers presented opportunities for Hitler and his ideologies of reunification of the German-speaking peoples of Europe. The establishment of the *Generalgouvernement* region from the former and now occupied Polish territory provided Hitler with a geographical solution to what was known as the 'Jewish question'. As early as 1936 the concept of establishing a Jewish state through the forced relocation of Jews from the Reich territories was being discussed. For a period, the island of Madagascar was identified as an ideal location, with Guyana serving as another potential option. However, the notion of the Jewish people forming a 'state' did not align with Hitler's preferences; he preferred to refer to any new settlement as a 'reservation', firmly under Nazi control. Essentially, the discussions among senior Nazis revolved around the concept of constructing a colossal open prison. Eventually, following political wrangling with Moscow, an area of land was identified in the former Polish territory between the San and Bug rivers, known as Nisko.

By early October 1939 Eichmann and the Central Office of Emigration in Vienna began formulating plans to initiate the deportation of Vienna's Jewish population to Nisko.[31] Dr Josef Löwenherz of the IKG was tasked with compiling a list of names of Jewish men eligible for transportation by 13 October. An advance party was to be despatched initially to construct a barracks capable of accommodating all those to be relocated. Naturally, the construction expenses were to be borne by IKG funds. Consequently, Dr Löwenherz was compelled to make the

[31]31. Dokumentationsarchiv des Österreichischen Widerstandes (Hrsg.), Forschungen zu Vertreibung und Holocaust, Wien 2018 (= Jahrbuch 2018) Winfried R. Garscha Deportation als Vertreibung Eichmanns Nisko-Experiment 1939 im Kontext der nationalsozialistischen, völkischen Flurbereinigung

first of numerous painful decisions that would profoundly impact his Jewish community: he was given only two days to provide a list of names of men eligible for transportation. He assembled a physically fit contingent from the Viennese community and provided them with comprehensive details, as far as he was led to believe, about the proposed resettlement of Jews in occupied Poland. As a result, he recruited volunteers to lead the construction of this new Jewish settlement. Approximately 830 mainly skilled men responded, many harbouring the misconception that they were being offered an opportunity to work and establish a fresh start, which was far from the reality.

Schaje Nussbaum, Anna's father, was one of the volunteers who participated in the transportation. As the outbreak of war and the subsequent closure of borders rendered his emigration application impractical, he joined a group of 912 men who boarded the first transport train to Nisko on 20 October 1939.

Both Schaje and Rebekka were born in the east Polish town of Gliniana which lies just sixty miles north-east of Nisko. With family roots in the general area, perhaps he thought that resettling at Nisko was his best option. Meanwhile, his wife Rebekka remained in Vienna, now occupying a *sammelwohnungen* or holding apartment at Odeongasse 5 in Vienna's second district ghetto area, having previously been evicted from their original Wehlistrasse home. This was a result of an order issued on 10 May 1939, which permitted landlords to terminate the tenancies of Jewish occupants, forcing them into ever more overcrowded housing. It was intended that the wives of the initial volunteers, including Rebekka, would follow in a subsequent transport and join their husbands in Nisko, with accommodation being constructed in the interim. This plan, however, did not materialise.

Adolf Eichmann sought to curry favour with Hitler and the senior Nazis. He perceived his Nisko plan as a means to fulfil a promise made to rid Vienna of Jews.[32] In his efforts to expedite

[32] Ibid.

the transports, he clashed with Reinhard Heydrich and Hans Frank, who were vying for power as military and civil leaders over the newly occupied territories. Military demands also prioritised the provision of rail transport. As a consequence, only three transports were ever made to Nisko, with the last departing Vienna on 29 October 1939. The women remained alone in Vienna, while the men were left to fend for themselves in the middle of winter in a desolate wasteland.

News of this latest development relating to the Jews in Europe had been stifled with the recent invasion of Poland and declarations of war. The *Belfast Newsletter*, however, carried a small column on 9 October 1939 which hinted at what was to follow; under the heading 'Jewish State In Poland' the report read:

> PARIS, Sunday - A plan of Hitler's to set up a Jewish state in Poland, where the Jews of the entire world would be gathered, was discussed during von Ribbentrop's visit to Moscow a few days ago, according to the Riga correspondent of the 'Paris Soir' today. The Soviet leaders offered no objection to the plan the correspondent adds. - Reuter.

Eight weeks later, the harsh realities of this newly-established Jewish state became evident. A well-informed report filed by American journalist Oswald Garrison Villard with *The Spectator* and subsequently carried by *The Liverpool Echo* on 5 December 1939 unveiled the fate of the initial Nisko transportees. The report foreshadowed the horrific circumstances that would befall the Jewish communities in Germany, Austria and Poland. Villard wrote:

> With practically no publication of the plan in the German newspapers Adolf Hitler is going ahead with the creation of a so-called Jewish State located in Poland, near Nisko on the San, south-west of Lublin.

> A stretch of land, about 50 by 60 miles in area, has been set aside. It Is enclosed by a barbed-wire fence, and only Jews will be allowed to live therein. Into this small territory are to be crammed no fewer than 1,945,000 Jews. What is to become of the Poles who have inhabited this region is not stated, but it is said in various quarters that the land is exceptionally poor.
>
> Whether it is poor or rich, this mass-migration by force has been begun now in the dead of winter, and in a manner that cannot be interpreted as anything else than a determination to create not a Jewish State, but a more horrible concentration camp which can certainly become nothing else than a habitation of death … .
>
> No preparations are made for their reception; they are simply to be dumped in and left to shift for themselves. If they cannot find shelter in the deserted homes of the evacuated Polish peasantry why, they can freeze to death, or build homes, without means, without materials, without tools, without any thing.
>
> How they are to subsist when they get there no one knows. How those who survive until the spring will obtain seeds and farming tools and cattle and horses no one can imagine. It is impossible to conceive of any more barbarous cruelty and it is deliberately calculated.
>
> Behind the barbed-wire fence the Jews are to live or die in circumstances which would not be permitted in any civilised country if the victims were dogs or cattle.

As an American, and with the USA not at that stage at war with Germany, Villard was still at liberty to gather such reports in Germany and beyond.

In contrast to the account provided, Schaje Nussbaum's circumstances were far more desperate. Given his proximity to his family, he made the decision to escape from Nisko. He embarked on a perilous journey on foot, constantly aware of the imminent threat posed by the SS-*Einsatzgruppen*, death squads formed by SS-Obergruppenführer Reinhard Heydrich. These death squads were tasked with implementing the Nazi regime's policy of ethnic cleansing in the newly-occupied territories, targeting for execution Poles, Jews and any individuals deemed 'undesirable'.

Schaje navigated the newly established territorial divide and found refuge in the Russian-occupied area, specifically in the town of Lemberg (Lviv). There, he managed to track down and sought shelter with his brother-in-law. Schaje managed to remain in Lviv until shortly after 22 June 1941 when Hitler reneged on his pact with Stalin, triggering the Nazi invasion of Russia, Operation Barbarossa.

In response to this escalating crisis, Schaje and his brother-in-law fled Lviv, which was swiftly captured by the German forces within a week. Seeking shelter, they approached a Polish farmer who, in exchange for a substantial cash payment, agreed to conceal the men. The farmer, after taking their money, betrayed Schaje and his brother-in-law to the SS-Einsatzgruppen. They were immediately detained by the SS, brought to the market square in Lviv and publicly murdered by being shot through the head. Rebekka, alone in Vienna, was left unaware of their plight.[33]

The hasty deportations of Vienna's Jews to Nisko were swiftly abandoned as, broadly speaking, the concept had proven

[33] Memoir book of Anna Nussbaum, later Chana Gross, born in Vienna, Austria in 1929, with inscriptions by her girlfriends in Vienna, Belfast and Millisle, Ireland and in London during 09/01/1939-17/07/1947, and her memoirs, Yad Vashem Archive, https://collections.yadvashem.org/en/documents/13417501 viewed 11/5/2025

disastrous. Drafted up in the wake of the war's outbreak, it faced opposition from Hans Frank, the newly appointed *Generalgouverneur* of the region, who vehemently opposed the establishment of a Jewish reservation on his territory. Regrettably, Eichmann, resolute in his mission to rid Vienna of Jews, reflected on the errors made and drew valuable lessons from them. He recognised that, from his perspective, certain aspects of the Nisko operation were successful; for instance, his managing to effectively compel Josef Löwenherz and his IKG staff to carry out the selection process. By doing so, he distanced the Nazi authorities from involvement in the unpleasant task of selection. This ultimately resulted in a side effect of having the Jews turn against their leaders, who were often accused of collaborating in their own demise.

The use of the IKG's files and various registrations of individuals and addresses to facilitate the selections and deportations was also successful. The system of corralling the selected individuals for transportation and the use of the railway network for their transportation were both well executed. In essence, Eichmann had developed and stress-tested meticulously the fundamental elements of a system that would later fulfil his requirements in addressing the 'Jewish question'. All he needed was time and another opportunity to implement what he had learned.

As the months passed in Vienna, the war presented new challenges to the already heavily subjugated Jewish community. The continued movement of families from their own and rented properties resulted in the formation of a loose ghetto within the second district. Food rationing and a ration card system were introduced. However, Eichmann compelled Löwenherz and the IKG to introduce their own ration system which was funded by ever depleting Jewish resources. The issue of ration cards was contingent upon a fresh nominal registration, effectively enabling the Gestapo, which oversaw the system, to continue to monitor the Jewish community as they were relocated from house to house within the city.

By the end of 1940, following further discussions between Hans Frank, Eichmann and Adolf Hitler himself, Eichmann finally achieved his objective: the transportation of Jews from Vienna to the *Generalgouvernement* region of the Reich, formerly Poland, was approved. Several towns with an existing Jewish population were identified for this purpose but no additional facilities were provided in each of these earmarked ghetto areas other than that the deportees were to be housed in the homes of the existing Jewish inhabitants or in community quarters such as halls and synagogues.

On 3 December 1940 Adolf Hitler authorised the deportation of the Jewish population of Vienna to the Generalgouvernement. On 1 February 1941, Eichmann implemented his revised plan to start the deportation of the remaining 60,000 Jewish individuals in the city, beginning with the deportation of 10,000 individuals in groups of 1,000. The following day, at 12 noon Löwenherz, Director of the IKG was summoned to the Central Office where, in the presence of SS-Obersturmführer Alois Brunner, he was given the following instructions by Dr Karl Ebner, head of the Jewish Section of the Vienna Gestapo. The instructions were in the form of thirteen points: the following relevant points have been translated from a copy of the original note relating to the meeting:

> Herr Councillor Dr Ebner disclosed the following information to me and gave me the following instructions:
>
> 1. It is planned to resettle some of the Jews living in Vienna to the General Government. The religious community (IKG) is to be kept out of this operation and will only have to carry out the instructions given to it. Approximately 1000 people are to be processed in one transport each. The first

> transport will depart on February 15, the second on February 19th 1941 and on every Wednesday of the following weeks. The time is still to be announced. The processing yard will probably be the Aspang railway station. It is intended to resettle 10,000 Jews to the General Government by May 1941. The settlement of the Jews in the Government will take place in small district towns. The names of these towns have not yet been announced.
>
> 2. The registration of Jews who are considered for allocation to individual transports is the responsibility of the Central Office for Jewish Emigration in accordance with decisions issued by higher authorities. Each traveller can carry 1 suitcase or 2 bales up to a maximum of 50kg in weight, in particular each emigrant should bring two good blankets and one good pair of shoes. In this regard the IKG should endeavour to ensure that Jews who have more shoes provide a pair to those who have not.

Points 3 and 4 related to matters in Yugoslavia. The document continued:

> 5. The selection of persons to be resettled in the General Government is carried out by the Central Office for Jewish Emigration in Vienna. The persons designated for the transport in question must lock their homes until they have been cleared by the Secret Police. The apartment numbers are to be handed over to the state authorities in Building II, 35 Castellezgasse. Each key must be provided with a cardboard tag. The apartment, the name of the apartment owner and his date of birth must be clearly marked on the tag.

The instructions went on to outline the procedures for the handing over of assets and belongings, explaining that the proceeds would be used to supplement the cost of the transfer and provision of food for the journey. The instructions contained the sinister caveat:

> If Jews do not voluntarily comply with the request of the Central Office for Jewish Emigration they will be brought before the police. In addition, these Jews must expect severe punishment.

Two Jewish schools, one located at Kleine Sperlgasse 2a, and another at Castellezgasse 35 in the second district, which had been increasingly accommodating teachers and pupils from other closed schools, were instructed to close. The schools' furnishings were removed, and they were both transformed into two *Sammellager*, or collection camps.

Using the information obtained from the housing and emigration registration forms, the IKG staff was forced to disseminate postcards to all individuals selected for deportation, instructing them to report to Kleine Sperlgasse 2a prior to their deportation. For a period of weeks, the school underwent a transformation into a concentration camp, similar to that observed by Gertrude Kessler at the rear of her apartment on Rauscherstrasse several months before. The IKG staff were made to call on those ordered to present themselves if they failed to attend on receipt of the postcard summons. If they still could not be found at their registered address the Gestapo then employed a tactic of sealing off the street in which they lived, usually at nighttime, and searching every property from end to end to flush out the occupants. As rumours of the impending deportations began to spread those who could hid in properties with others not yet ordered to leave or with non-Jewish friends. In the case of the latter, these instances were very rare. Gertrude

Kessler recounted to her grandson Charlie years later that many attempted to hide within undergrowth in the city parks; regulations were later imposed banning Jews from parks altogether and from walking the streets at night.

In response to this new development, the Society of Friends, with a staff of only three individuals, changed their policy from helping individuals emigrate to preparing them for imminent deportation. Given their limited resources, they provided essential support, including food and warm clothing for the journey and the uncertain future that awaited them.[34]

The first transport from Vienna departed on 15 February 1941 to Opole in occupied Poland, followed by two more transports in February, one to Kielce and another to Opole. Each transport train endeavoured to accommodate 1,000 individuals who had been previously assembled at the repurposed school. Transport number 4 was scheduled to depart on 5 March 1941. Ernestine and Leopold Kessler received instructions to report to Kleine Sperlgasse where they attended and were joined by Rebekka Nussbaum, who was now alone. Her daughter, Anni, had been evacuated to Millisle along with Gertrude and Fritz Kessler while her husband had been murdered in Lviv without her knowledge. Helene König was also summoned to attend from her residence at the nursing home on Seegasse 9; like Rebekka Nussbaum, she was unaware of the whereabouts of her husband or for that matter, her 8-year-old daughter, Felicitas. Paul Messinger was also ordered to the school; he obeyed along with his wife Erna.

Upon arrival at Kleine Sperlgasse, the deportees underwent a thorough processing procedure supervised by Josef Löwenherz's IKG staff, accompanied and closely overlooked by five or six Gestapo officers. Each deportee was required to surrender the keys to their property, attached to a cardboard label bearing the address. All monetary assets and valuables were handed over;

[34] *Stemming The Dark Tide*, Sheila Spielhofer, Sessions of York, ISBN 1 85072 267 6

other possessions were restricted to two suitcases with a total weight limit of 50 kilograms.

Upon the complete surrender of cash, an account was opened for each individual, accompanied by a statement. For Leopold and Ernestine Kessler, the bank statement remains in existence and is preserved in the Yad Vashem archive in Jerusalem. The reference number for the account is IV/129,130, which corresponds to their passenger numbers on Transport No. 4 or IV.

The statement indicates that a sum of 20 Reichsmarks was deposited into each account and subsequently converted into 80 Zloty (Polish currency). Regardless of the amount taken from them, this constituted the sole compensation provided to each passenger. The robbery of the Jewish people continued.

All ration cards and passports, if still in possession, were ordered to be handed over to the Gestapo officers. The officers revelled in the terrified deportees' reactions as the precious documents were torn up in front of their eyes. This act served as a clear indication that there was no return and no further need for passports. Each individual was assigned a transport number. For transport number 4, the numbers ranged from 1 to 999. A list was compiled for each transport, containing the names, dates of birth and corresponding numbers. The primary reason for this was that the IKG was invoiced by the *Reichsbahn* or German Railways for each individual fare. In effect, the Jews were compelled to pay for their own forced deportation. Once processed, the deportees were forced to wait, in most cases for days, in the sparse rooms of the vacant school. Having been robbed of their possessions and hope, many at this point resorted to suicide.

In the case of transport number 4, the total number of passengers listed was 999. This number should have been 1000, suggesting that one individual had taken his or her own life before the train departed. Alternatively, it is possible that one person listed to travel was an IKG staff member, and their deportation was delayed as they were deemed an essential worker after making representations to the IKG processing staff.

The Quakers continued to provide assistance to those who sought their help and found themselves awaiting deportation at the school in Kleine Sperlgasse. By late February 1941 Grete Sumpf, one of the remaining Friends providing assistance from the Vienna centre, received letters from individuals who had been deported on the first and second transports to Opole and Kielce.[35] On learning of the deplorable conditions and overcrowding in both locations, she resolved to provide practical support for those ordered to be transported. She appealed to the German office of the Society of Friends in Berlin and promptly obtained packages of warm clothing and materials which were sorted into piles by a sewing circle group she organised composed of individuals threatened with deportation. Quilts were constructed and warm clothing was repaired, which were distributed to those who presented themselves at Sperlgasse and who lacked the financial means to provide such items due to the relentless deprivation they were experiencing. She recognised that simple items, such as old curtains, could be used to wrap around feet and provide protection from the extreme cold encountered in the ghetto towns.

Of the 999 deportees listed for Transport No.4, 312 of them were over the age of 61, with an average age of 49. Unlike the Nisko operation conducted by Eichmann, both men and women were transported, as well as entire families, including married couples such as the Kesslers and Messingers, individuals of all ages, including single mothers with young babies and toddlers. Many of whom were already in a state of profound desperation even before March 1941.

A notable case is that of Nanette Kac, a 39-year-old teacher, who lost her job in 1939 due to the implementation of the Nuremberg Laws. Her husband was arrested and detained in

---

[35] *Stemming The Dark Tide*, Sheila Spielhofer, Sessions of York, ISBN 1 85072 267 6

Buchenwald Camp on 13 September 1939, leaving Nanette and their 3-year-old daughter to fend for themselves in the chaotic Vienna.

Nanette successfully obtained an emigration visa to the United States with the assistance of her brother-in-law, a resident of New York, who provided an affidavit for her, her husband, and their daughter, Renate. Since her husband Zyskind's incarceration in September 1939, Nanette repeatedly wrote to the IKG to request Zyskind's release so that they could emigrate together. In her final letter, she expressed her destitution and dependency on the IKG for her survival while awaiting the possibility of Zyskind being released despite having a valid visa from October 1939.

Nanette was forced to reside in a *Sammellager* apartment at Grosse Sperlgasse, located near the former school at Kleine Sperlgasse. Hearing no word regarding the release of her husband, she was left with no choice but to join the others along with her daughter, on Transport No.4 for deportation on 5 March 1941. The last recorded information regarding her husband, Zyskind, states that he was transferred from Buchenwald to Ravensbrück Concentration Camp the following year on 14 March 1942, Ravensbrück having been designated as a site for executions from 1941 onwards.

One of the other Quaker-assisted deportees was 70-year-old Jolante Spohrer. Jolante had been relocated to a *Sammellwohnungen* housing block that accommodated over fifty-six individuals in twelve apartments prior to her move to Kleine Sperlgasse. Grete Sumpf had previously discussed the prospect of deportation with Jolante and was impressed by her positive attitude, which was evident as one of the more senior deportees.[36] As the departure dates approached, Grete discovered that the majority of the individuals sought only the comfort and re-assurance of a conversation. Many had resigned themselves to their fate, even though they were still not fully aware of the implications.

---

[36] Ibid.

On 5 March 1941 the 999 deportees were loaded onto lorries at Kleine Sperlgasse by Gestapo guards. Their baggage was taken from them and loaded separately and they were then driven through the streets of Vienna on a five-mile journey, taking around fifteen minutes to arrive at the Aspang railway station. En route the trucks were attacked by the Viennese locals, now well aware of who they were and where they were being taken. On arrival at the Aspang station they were herded off the lorries and onto the carriages of a waiting train, one hundred people per carriage.

Aspang station was usually reserved for freight railway traffic with generally no foot passengers arriving or leaving. The station was overlooked by Viennese housing blocks, four- and five-storey buildings which afforded the many occupants a grandstand view of all that went on. The deportees were afforded no privacy as they unceremoniously boarded their carriages, prodded and goaded by Gestapo guards. They took their final steps off Viennese soil, watched from above by people amongst whom they had lived, worked alongside, dealt with and played with as they went about their lives, and who now glared at them as they were forced to leave their home city.

Today, the Aspangbahnhof station no longer exists. Instead, a memorial stands in its place, overlooked by the surrounding buildings that were there in 1941. This memorial honours the 60,000 individuals who took their final steps from that very spot. In September 2024, the author visited the memorial with Charlie Warmington. The monument constructed in the station's place is a striking representation of the original railway tracks, formed by two almost converging concrete lines. These lines appear to converge and disappear within a dark tunnel, symbolising the ominous fate that awaited the passengers departing from that location. The railway continues to operate alongside the site, with trains passing by frequently as Charlie stood there, contemplating the events that played out at this place and the fear experienced by his grandparents and countless other ordinary individuals as they vanished from sight into an inky darkness.

Charlie Warmington cleans the headstone marking his grandmother's grave at the Feuerhalle Simmering burial ground in Vienna.

The details on the headstone revealing that Charlie's grandmother's remains were buried along with those of the man who protected her, Karl Piekarowitz and his wife Marie Helene.

The original Kessler family home at Leystrasse 23 in Vienna's 20th District.

The Stolpersteine (stumbling stones) memorial stones installed outside the final apartment occupied by the Kessler family at Streffleurgasse 4 in Vienna's 20th District prior to their deportation. Over 1000 of these brass memorials have been installed in Vienna. Each stone commemorates an individual at the very place where they lived, were taken from or forced into exile.

Image taken by a Nazi at Kleine Sperlegasse, where jews were loaded onto lorries and deported after being held at the repurposed school building at Kleine Sperlegasse 2 (Source WStLA).

Charlie standing at the exact location shown in the previous picture, where his grandparents were loaded onto lorries prior to their departure on Transport No.4 after being held at the repurposed school building at Kleine Sperlegasse 2.

A happy school memory drawn by Gertrude on the inner cover of the "Deutsches Kochbuch" or German cookbook given to her by her mother Ernestine prior to being evacuated from Vienna. (Courtesy of the Warmington family.)

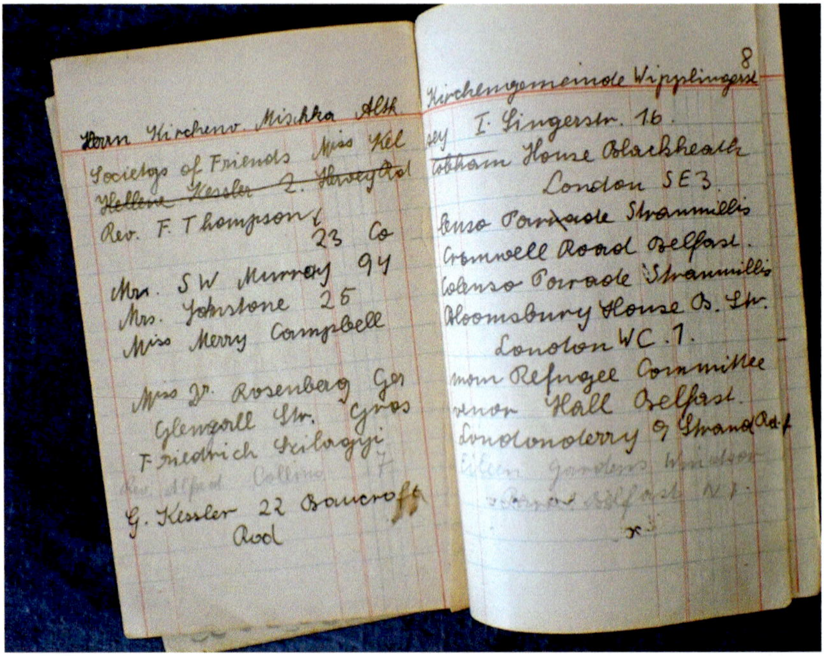

Inside the cookbook, among the various recipes, were the names and contact details of those who could help her during her Kindertransport evacuation. (Courtesy of the Warmington family.)

Charlie takes in the scene and the memorial erected today at the former site of Aspangbahnhof railway station. Between October 1939 and October 1942, approximately 50,000 individuals were forcibly rounded up and transported from the station that stood here to ghettos, concentration camps, and ultimately extermination camps.

Looking for evidence at the empty photographic studio that belonged to Karl Piekarowitz at Rauscherstrasse 4 in Vienna. Charlie's grandmother Ernestine Kessler went into hiding at these premises for over three years until the city was liberated by the Soviet Army in 1945.

The photograph of Ernestine Kessler taken by Karl Piekarowitz at his studio in February 1942. (Courtesy of the Warmington family.)

The rear of the photograph sent by Ernestine with the message designed to reassure her children Gertrude and Fritz. (Courtesy of the Warmington family.)

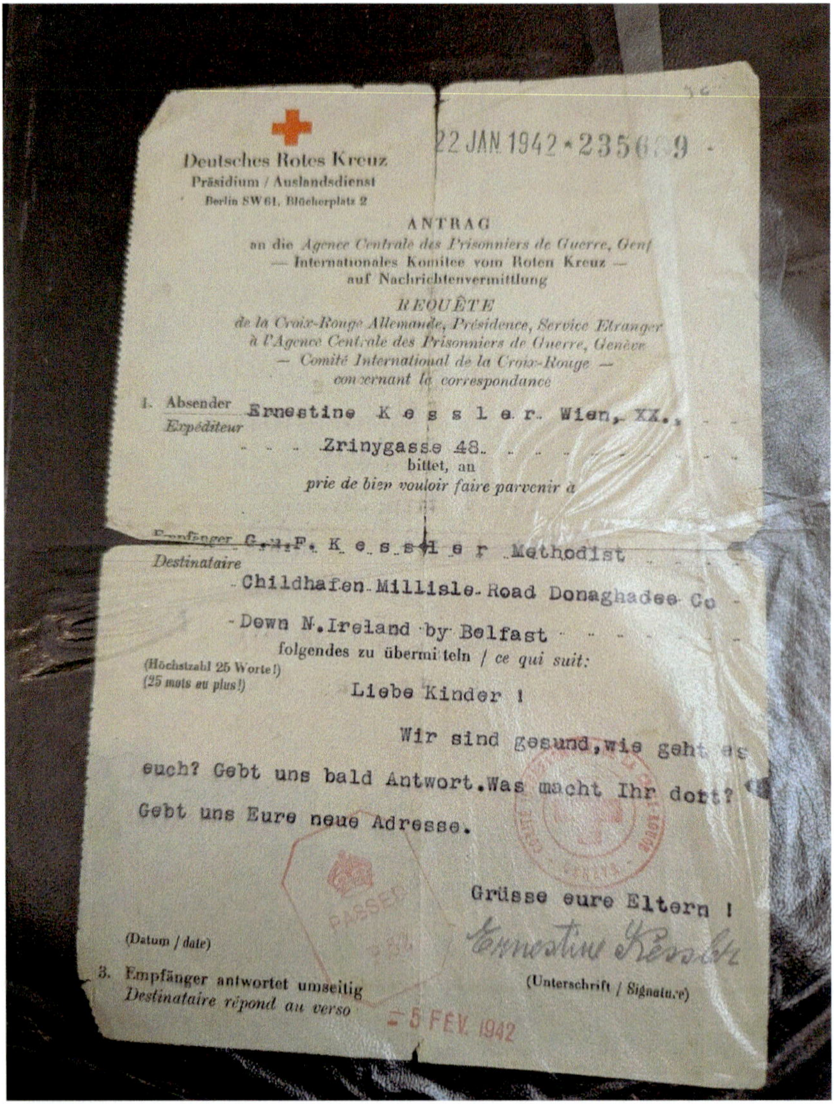

22 JAN 1942 * 2356[illegible]9

Deutsches Rotes Kreuz
Präsidium / Auslandsdienst
Berlin SW 61, Blücherplatz 2

ANTRAG
an die *Agence Centrale des Prisonniers de Guerre, Genf*
— Internationales Komitee vom Roten Kreuz —
auf Nachrichtenvermittlung

REQUÊTE
de la Croix-Rouge Allemande, Présidence, Service Etranger
à l'Agence Centrale des Prisonniers de Guerre, Genève
— Comité International de la Croix-Rouge —
concernant la correspondance

1. Absender / *Expéditeur* Ernestine Kessler. Wien, XX., Zrinygasse 48.
bittet, an
prie de bien vouloir faire parvenir à

Empfänger / *Destinataire* G. F. Kessler Methodist Childhafen Millisle Road Donaghadee Co Down N.Ireland by Belfast
folgendes zu übermitteln / *ce qui suit:*
(Höchstzahl 25 Worte!)
(25 mots au plus!)

Liebe Kinder !

Wir sind gesund, wie geht es euch? Gebt uns bald Antwort. Was macht Ihr dort? Gebt uns Eure neue Adresse.

Grüsse eure Eltern !

Ernestine Kessler

(Datum / *date*)

(Unterschrift / Signature)

3. Empfänger antwortet umseitig
Destinataire répond au verso

PASSED

- 5 FEV. 1942

The folded German Red Cross message sent from Vienna to her children in Millisle by Ernestine Kessler while she was in hiding in Vienna. Courtesy of the Warmington family.

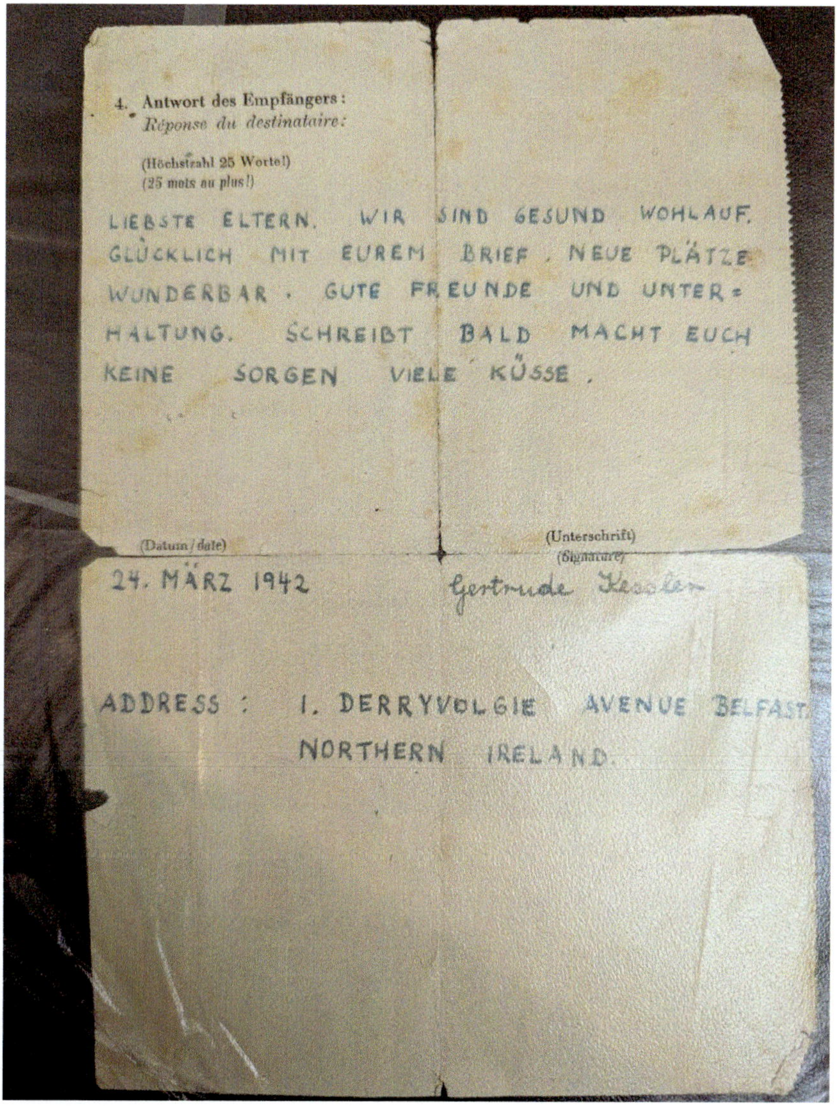

4. **Antwort des Empfängers:**
Réponse du destinataire:

(Höchstzahl 25 Worte!)
(25 mots au plus!)

LIEBSTE ELTERN. WIR SIND GESUND WOHLAUF. GLÜCKLICH MIT EUREM BRIEF. NEUE PLÄTZE WUNDERBAR. GUTE FREUNDE UND UNTER=HALTUNG. SCHREIBT BALD MACHT EUCH KEINE SORGEN VIELE KÜSSE.

(Datum/date)
24. MÄRZ 1942

(Unterschrift)
(Signature)
Gertrude Kessler

ADDRESS: 1. DERRYVOLGIE AVENUE BELFAST NORTHERN IRELAND.

The rear of the Red Cross message with the return message sent by Gertrude from Belfast. This message was returned to Belfast a second time with the photograph of Ernestine enclosed. (Courtesy of the Warmington family.

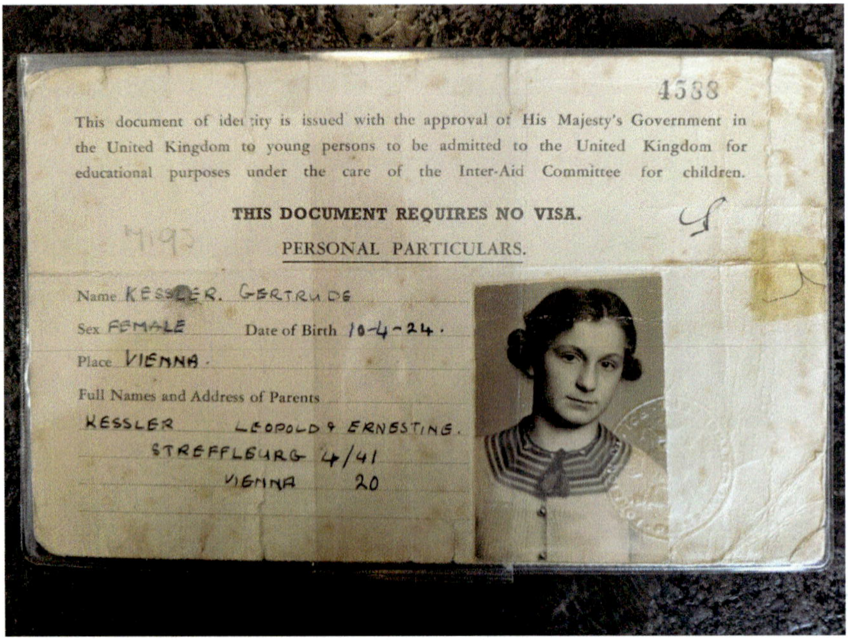

4588

This document of identity is issued with the approval of His Majesty's Government in the United Kingdom to young persons to be admitted to the United Kingdom for educational purposes under the care of the Inter-Aid Committee for children.

THIS DOCUMENT REQUIRES NO VISA.

PERSONAL PARTICULARS.

Name KESSLER. GERTRUDE

Sex FEMALE Date of Birth 10-4-24.

Place VIENNA.

Full Names and Address of Parents

KESSLER LEOPOLD & ERNESTINE.

STREFFLEURG 4/41

VIENNA 20

Gertrude's identity card and photograph. The rear of the card was certified by a sergeant at Bangor RUC station. (Courtesy of the Warmington family.)

The Schrekinger family circa 1915 including Josef Brunner and Anton Vogelsang in Austro-Hungarian military uniform. The others in the photograph, from left to right are Anna, Berta, Rosa, Anna (senior), Eleonore and Charlie's grandmother, Ernestine. (Courtesy of the Warmington family.)

On the following page are Gestapo detention photographs of Anna, Anton and Josef.

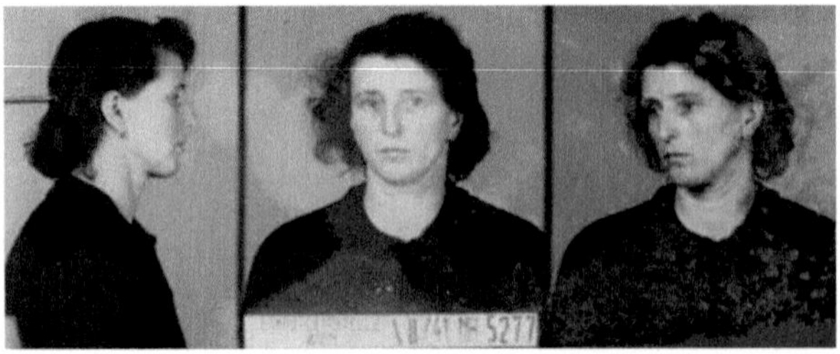

Vienna Gestapo detention photograph taken of Eleonore Vogelsang nee Schrekinger showing likely evidence of maltreatment with bruising around her eyes. Source: WStLA. WStLA, Gestapo, K1 Gestapo File: Eleonore Vogelsang, born February 2, 1898.

Vienna Gestapo detention photograph. Source WStLA. WStLA, Gestapo, K1 Gestapo File: Anton Vogelsang, born December 14, 1898.

Vienna Gestapo detention photograph. Source WStLA. WStLA, Gestapo, K1 Gestapo File: Josef Brenner, born January 26, 1890.

The final resting place and memorial to the murdered Communist Resistance Fighters Fritz Zwickl, Franz Reinelt, Matthias Nagel, Anton Vogelsang, Josef Brenner and Otto Wehofschitz at the Feuerhalle Simmering burial ground in Vienna.

Charlie Warmington in Augarten Park close to one of the Nazi flak towers dominating the area.

Paul Messinger with his wife and four sons taken in Hiafa, Israel on the occasion of his son Daniel's wedding in 1992. From right to left: Michael (son), Paul Messinger, Daniel (son), Gabriel (son), Simha (wife) and son Raphael. (Photo courtesy of Daniel Messinger, Haifa, Israel.)

CHAPTER 5

Modliborzyce - "Aktion Reinhardt"

After a journey lasting two full days and nights, the Transport No.4 train arrived at the eastern Polish railway station of Szastarka on 7 March 1941. From there, the exhausted, hungry and bewildered deportees were transported by horse-drawn cart or on foot to a small settlement some 15 kilometres further south in the Lublin District, known as Modliborzyce, their intended new residence. Many of those deported held the belief, and were indeed informed in a similar manner to their earlier Nisko predecessors, that they could establish a community in the areas in which they were resettled, find employment, construct homes, and continue their lives. However, this was merely another of a continuous stream of lies devised to facilitate compliance with the deportation process. What awaited them at Modliborzyce was the stark and painful reality that they had, in effect, been sentenced to a slow death.

The settlement, situated approximately fifty kilometres south of the regional capital of Lublin, had been the target of German air raids just eighteen months before, during the Nazi-Soviet invasion of Poland. Between 8 and 15 September 1939, the Luftwaffe bombed Modliborzyce twice during operations related to the battle of Tomaszów Lubelski, resulting in the deaths of eighty-seven inhabitants.[37] The majority of the village's central area and numerous dwelling houses were destroyed and had not been rebuilt; indeed Jewish owners of destroyed properties were forbidden to carry out any reconstruction.

The existing Jewish community, whose population, according to local council records, numbered 1,300 in 1939, represented some 40 per cent of the total population. Overnight, with the influx of the Vienna deportees, this figure almost doubled and, with a separate arrival of evacuees from Poznan and Prague, the total Jewish population reached approximately 2,500 inhabitants. Unlike other resettled towns and areas of cities to where Jews were deported, there was no sole Jewish quarter or ghetto in Modliborzyce. The original Jewish Poles lived alongside and among their non-Jewish neighbours. Furthermore, the layout of the village meant that it was impossible to seal off any particular section of the settlement to form a ghetto without disrupting through traffic and the everyday business for the remainder.

The sudden influx of people posed significant challenges. The local Jewish Council self-help group had already been under pressure to accommodate the increased population caused by displaced individuals from local villages affected by the war. Despite representations made to their higher authority in Krakow, additional funding was not forthcoming to provide food and essentials for the new arrivals. Indeed, only two days' notice had been provided for the arrival of the Viennese Jews, leaving no time to prepare for their needs.[38]

---

[37] History of the Commune Modliborzyce.
https://bibliotekaukazimierza.pl/aktualnosci/1163-z-kart-historii-gminy-modliborzyce.html viewed 11/5/2025

[38] Ibid.

Furthermore, when Transport No.4 departed Aspangbahnhof on 5 March, the final two carriages had not been coupled to the train. Those carriages contained the personal belongings of the passengers, their suitcases and bundles containing clothing and bedding. The deportees arrived in a remote location with only the clothes they were wearing.

Back in Vienna, and on discovering this error, Josef Löwenherz of the IKG promptly notified Eichmann's Central Office. Initially, the Central Office declined to take any action, but, after persistent representations, the baggage cars were subsequently forwarded, arriving five days later. It is difficult to avoid the conclusion that the failure to couple, or the uncoupling of, the baggage cars was another instance of deliberate cruelty perpetrated by the SS guards.

On 7 March 1941, upon his arrival at the station at Sastarka, Viennese dentist Dr Alfred Kneucker, a deportee on Transport No.4, managed to send a telegram to his wife, who was still residing at their home on Wahringerstrasse 93 in Vienna.[39] The telegram briefly stated, 'Arrived safely – Papa – Modliborzyce near Krasnik', suggesting that the destination was not communicated to the deportees prior to their departure. He sent a further postcard that evening, indicating that he had arrived in a hurry and that the location was near Lublin. He assured his wife Josefine that he would provide further details in a later telegram.

On 13 March he again wrote to his wife, describing the devastating impact on the people due to the delay in the delivery of their luggage. He wrote:

> The thing that was tormenting me, the constant worry about the luggage, is over. I also got the second suitcase so nothing was lost. But it is almost

[39] Documentation Centre of Austrian Resistance, https://www.doew.at/erinnern/fotos-und-dokumente/1938-1945/nachrichten-aus-dem-ghetto/modliborzyce/alfred-kneucker-verliert-die-psyche-die-haltung

> impossible to describe how the whole thing went down. Around 4000 suitcases – plus a screaming, gesticulating, nervous crowd of around 1100 people whipped up around the little bit of stuff – an inferno of Dante! But these people have the way of only thinking of themselves – a bit like after a play when people all push their way together at the same time, so that the distribution of the suitcases takes more than a week! I waited calmly and got everything without screaming.

The frenzy instilled in the crowd is understandable when one considers the conditions into which those people were thrust. What Dr Kneucker omitted from his letter was the fact that, when the deportees eventually arrived at Modliborzyce, there was no accommodation set aside for them to occupy. The synagogue was opened hastily and provided cramped shelter for only sixty people, in damp conditions on a stone floor without bedding. A building attached to the synagogue containing four small rooms provided shelter for a further forty-eight people; another fifteen were put up in a single room measuring just 3 by 4 metres. For everyone else, 876 people, there was nothing in the ruined settlement for them but an open field. Those conditions remained for a period of two weeks during which time the Viennese arrivals were forced to remain exposed to the elements with little food and in harsh weather conditions. The local population, both Jewish and non-Jewish, although sympathetic to the plight of the newcomers, were prohibited from offering them shelter in their own homes until authorisation arrived two weeks after their arrival. By that stage, many of the Viennese had inevitably succumbed to serious illness, posing a significant challenge for Dr Kneucker and the other twenty-one doctors and medical professionals who had arrived on board Transport No.4, Paul Messinger among them, and the existing Modliborzyce doctor attached to the Jewish Council or *Judenrat,* Dr Seeman.

The medical crisis also presented an additional opportunity for the Nazis to exploit a situation they had created and rob Jews of any remaining money or valuables.

In Kwaitkowice, close to Krasnik, a medical centre was available and authorised to treat Jews from the Janów district. By early April, arrangements had been made to allow a number of sick Viennese patients to receive treatment at this facility, typically those suffering from pneumonia, circulatory disorders and also infectious diseases, all attributable to the living conditions they were forced to endure. The medical fees imposed on the Judenrat amounted to 800 zloty; even with some of the patients paying from their own funds, this bill eradicated the entire Jewish Council self-help medical budget. The Judenrat attempted to admit a single patient for treatment in April but the admission was refused as the previous outstanding medical bill had not been paid.[40]

Dr Seeman was assisted in the small medical centre at Modliborzyce by a nurse who had arrived with her husband on Transport No. 4. Irma Wollner and her husband, Siegfried, passenger numbers 450 and 451 respectively, had originally lived in Vienna's 15th district at 31 Reichsapfelgasse. At the age of 58, Irma was an experienced nurse and, on arriving in the settlement and witnessing the unfolding humanitarian disaster, she volunteered to assist the community doctor in the poorly equipped medical centre.

The twenty-two doctors and medical staff immediately began attending to both the sick who had arrived from Vienna and the population of Modliborzyce and beyond. Despite their expertise, they lacked essential medicines and equipment, rendering their efforts largely ineffective.

Within a few months, an epidemic of typhus began to spread, exacerbated by the unsanitary living conditions, cramped and

---

[40] History of the Commune Modliborzyce. https://bibliotekaukazimierza.pl/aktualnosci/1163-z-kart-historii-gminy-modliborzyce.html viewed 11/5/2025

overcrowded accommodations and infestations of lice. The exact date of the disease's manifestation is uncertain since the Nazi authorities prohibited the official reporting of the disease by the Modliborzyce medical centre, thereby hindering any appropriate and effective medical response.

A report made in autumn 1941 by Dr Sowiakowski, the director of the Janów Lubelski District Hospital, located just seven kilometres away from the community, stated that 'only 700 Austrian citizens of Jewish origin remained'.[41] He specifically mentioned the medical staff, noting that 'fourteen doctors, including three professors at the [Austrian University] faculty of medicine, have survived'.

Clearly, the doctors and medical staff were not immune to contracting the diseases they were attempting to eradicate; nevertheless, their professional ethics compelled them to continue to assist those in need and they did not remain idle. Nurse Irma Wollner succumbed to disease and died in the settlement on 8 January 1942. She was buried in a communal grave in the Jewish cemetery at Modliborzyce. The cemetery site still remains today but there are no longer any headstones to mark the graves of the Viennese deportees, all the grave markers having been destroyed in an act of vandalism by the Nazis. Recently, archaeological work was carried out at the cemetery site, and the broken remains of one unidentifiable headstone was discovered – nothing else.

In less than eight months, the twenty-two medical professionals had lost eight of their colleagues, resulting in a fatality percentage comparable to that of the entire Transport No. 4 community. Written accounts of the conditions endured in Modliborzyce are scarce. Letters and postcards could be sent from the settlement via the operational postal system at that time. Unfortunately, as numerous entire families were deported together, and relatives at home were frequently displaced, there were few individuals with whom anyone could correspond. The

[41] Ibid.

surviving correspondence provides a stark portrayal of a bleak existence, characterised by a perpetual struggle to procure food and clean water and the gradual deprivation and eventual demise of many of the occupants in living conditions reminiscent of medieval times.

Dr Alfred Kneucker wrote a number of letters to his wife Josefine. They mostly concerned his efforts in having his dentistry equipment sent to him in order that he could continue to practise at Modliborzyce; importantly this gave him a source of income as well as providing a service to the community. Then, in March 1942, Josefine Kneucker received a letter from Modliborzyce dated the 9th. It was written by Siegfried Wollner, the husband of nurse Irma Wollner. In his introduction, he recounted how his wife Irma had passed away on 8 January. However, he proceeded to inform Josefine her that her husband, Alfred, had succumbed to an illness in his care the previous evening. This revelation revealed that Siegfried had also assumed a nursing role within the community.[42]

He then went on to describe how he had met Alfred at Kleine Sperlgasse school in Vienna prior to their forced deportation. From that moment on, they had developed a close friendship.

It is believed that Alfred Kneucker passed away at the nearby hospital in Kwiatkowice. The official cause of his death was recorded as angina, although the underlying cause, suppressed by the authorities, may have been typhoid. The following morning Alfred's body was transported from the hospital to the cemetery in Modliborzyce. Siegfried Wollner personally ensured that, under the circumstances, the Jewish burial rites were observed and accompanied the body from the time of death. He lowered the doctor's coffin into the grave and remained at the graveside until it was covered with soil.

---

[42] Documentation Centre of Austrian Resistance, https://www.doew.at/erinnern/fotos-und-dokumente/1938-1945/nachrichten-aus-dem-ghetto/modliborzyce/alfred-kneucker-verliert-die-psyche-die-haltung

By all accounts, Siegfried Wollner was a virtuous individual. Despite the loss of his wife and the unimaginable hardships he endured under impossible circumstances, he retained his strength of character to ensure that his newfound friend was treated with dignity in his final days. His burial was conducted with the utmost respect under the most trying conditions

Tragically, within nine months of writing his letter to Alfred Kneucker's widow, Siegfried Wollner met his own demise. In fact, the process and method of his murder were already underway at that time in March 1942. Siegfried Wollner does not have a marked grave, nor was he afforded any respect in death but, as we shall discover, he did not die alone.

Another letter was sent from Modliborzyce to Grete Sumpf, still assisting whoever she could from The Society of Friends at Singerstrasse in Vienna. The letter came from Jolante Spohrer who had been assigned number 604 on Transport No.4. Jolante was 76 years old in 1941 and had been deported alone. In the weeks before her deportation, she had been helped by Grete. Jolante's message was alarmingly short and to the point:[43]

> As my only pair of shoes is finished, I turn to you with confidence. Above all, I need a pair of snow shoes, size 43. We are suffering great deprivation. In God's name, do not forget us!

In internal correspondence Grete noted that, prior to her deportation, Jolante had shown great courage and humour, and it was believed that she could come to terms with these most difficult of circumstances. However, she had 'Obviously found the conditions much more difficult than she had expected'.

At the age of 71, Hermine Kubie was also deported alone without family, as passenger number 266. Her son Alfons had previously managed to escape from Vienna to Geneva,

---

[43] *Stemming The Dark Tide*, Sheila Spielhofer, Sessions of York, ISBN 1 85072 267 6

Switzerland, in 1938. Hermine maintained regular correspondence with him while incarcerated at Modliborzyce. From the outset her postcards described vividly the desperate situation, including severe food shortages, escalating prices for available sustenance and the daily occurrence of deaths and burials. Hermine survived by organising packages to be sent to her, co-ordinated by Alfons, from various relatives who were able to assist. She successfully negotiated bartering items she had received for other food items but relied heavily on the provisions from outside the settlement. In September 1941 she informed her son that she was engaging in the sale of certain goods he had sent her and was saving the proceeds. Her postcard dated 13 September 1941 provided further details:[44]

> I have now received all three packages from Lisbon and thank you very much for them, the first was three boxes of sardines, the second was one can of honey, I think, and the third was cacao with sugar. It's a shame that I didn't get any cheese, it was so good. I'll keep the honey, the other will be sold, I have to save money now, because I have a plan. I don't want to stay here any more winters, the doctor said that old sickly people cannot survive the harsh winter here and should find somewhere else to go.

What was Hermine's plan that was so important that she was prepared to sell valuable food items to prepare for it? Who was the doctor she had spoken to? Obviously, she had to be guarded with her writing as a postcard could be read by anyone along its route. Was she indicating that there was a way to escape from Modliborzyce?

---

[44] Documentation Centre of Austrian Resistance, ://www.doew.at/erinnern/fotos-und-dokumente/1938-1945/nachrichten-aus-dem-ghetto/modliborzyce/hermine-kubie-um-jahrhunderte-zurueck

We know little of how Ernestine and Leopold Kessler fared at Modliborzyce. They sent a short letter to Gertrude and Fritz, facilitated by the Society of Friends, immediately after their *Kindertransport* departure in April 1939 when they were still living in Vienna to exchange addresses, but nothing was sent later to their children to indicate that they had been deported to Poland. Perhaps they didn't want overly to concern their children, having promised that they would soon see them again.

Post-war records reveal that Leopold Kessler became a member of the Judenrat in Modliborzyce. However, he is listed as a road-worker until the end of 1941 but it is plausible that he assumed a Judenrat role after 1941 as a means of security, perhaps in a management position with the road-working forced-labour parties. Able-bodied men were segregated from women and the elderly on a daily basis and used as slave labour. They were employed in road construction and quarrying operations, operating from two work camps located near Lysakow and Jenisow.

The separation of men from the settlement and their frequent absence during the day rendered Modliborzyce vulnerable to raids by SS-Einsatzgruppen death squads accompanied by Gendarmerie. Searches for partisans was the pretext for these raids, but they frequently resulted in robbery, assault and murder. There is no doubt that Modliborzyce had become a dangerous environment for a number of reasons, but what of the possibility of escape? Hermine Kubie wrote again to her son in Geneva on 10 October 1941. Among her pleas for food parcels and expressing horror at the escalating costs, she made another interesting remark:

> Unfortunately everything has gotten worse, so that I have had to abandon my plan again for an indefinite period. I wanted to save up for it, but you can never have enough money here.

It was evident that Hermione had discovered a plan to escape which necessitated financial resources, an expense which she was unwilling to provide, given her inability to sustain herself. On 18 October, she wrote to Alfons once more, disclosing on this occasion another piece of information relating to her abandoned plan:

> First of all, I gave up my trip for many reasons and must be content to arrange my life here as best I can for the time being. This is not for old people, they had to walk 50 kilometres and the Gr has not written yet, who knows whether he arrived.

The identity of 'GR' and the significance of the underlining of the word 'whether' remain unknown. Upon analysing each element of her comments, we can deduce the following: there was a potential escape route from Modliborzyce, albeit at a substantial financial cost and involving a fifty-kilometre trek, which would be physically demanding for the elderly and undernourished, especially during winter. The reference to 'GR' and the plural 'they' who had already undertaken this journey suggest that escape attempts had already been made before 18 October 1941, implying the possibility of an established 'lifeline' back to civilisation. By late 1941, there emerged a glimmer of hope that individuals with determination, courage and of sufficient physical fitness could successfully escape Modliborzyce and return to Vienna. Hermine Kubie carefully assessed the odds and, understandably, at 71 years of age, opted to remain in her existing situation.

In contrast, Ernestine Kessler, aged 39, who had a family far away, and another friend from Transport No.4, passenger number 870, Helene König, aged 51, who was also motivated to find her missing husband and daughter, chose to play the hand they had been dealt and attempt to escape from the ghetto.

For Helene the choice was simple: all she needed, apart from money, was the courage to get on with it. Failure and capture en route undoubtedly meant death, either instantly, shot wherever she was found, or lingering in a concentration camp which was in effect what was happening to them where they were. For Ernestine the decision to escape was more complicated: how could she leave her husband? What would Leopold do? Unfortunately, we do not know what whispered conversations went on in some corner of a stinking, overcrowded room or behind a wall in a biting wind to avoid eavesdroppers. We are not privy to the rationale, and nor can we even place ourselves in their shoes at that time and see perhaps that there was only one choice to make, similar to their decision to send off Gertrude and Fritz on the Kindertransport. Perhaps money was the deciding factor: maybe only one could afford to go or maybe Leopold's position in the Judenrat offered him hope of a better chance of survival. Whatever the reasoning, we have no idea how the decision was made, but it was decided that Ernestine would make the break with Helene and leave without her husband Leopold.

There is a statistic that one comes across in researching the history of Transport Number 4; it is that out of the 999 people who left Vienna on board that train on 5 March 1941 only thirteen survived. Though researching this subject I cannot find a definitive list of those thirteen survivors, I have no doubt that one exists. What I can say is that unless you were a doctor or you physically escaped from Modliborzyce, there was no final expectation of survival. There is also a question over the definition of 'survive'. Is it to survive to the next camp, survive the Holocaust or live a full life in peace? Each of those concepts is open to debate. What I know now and am certain of is that, if Ernestine and Helene remained where they were, they were destined to be murdered.

If we categorise those who made the audacious attempt to escape from Modliborzyce, they could be divided into two distinct groups: those who had everything to gain, such as

Ernestine Kessler and Helene König, who were seeking their children, and those who had nothing to lose. Records exist of an attempt made by a single individual during this period, who fell into the second category, that of having nothing to left to lose.

Oskar Weiss originally came from Sarajevo in what was known then as Yugoslavia.[45] Oskar moved to Vienna and lived in an apartment at Rögergasse 3 in the 9th District; his wife, Rosalina (née Cohen), was a patient in the care home of the 14th District Am Steinhof, Baumgartner Hoehe, which was an adult psychiatric hospital in Vienna, later known as the Otto Wagner Hospital. Following the *Anschluss* Adolf Hitler determined that the Steinhof Hospital would become the centre of National Socialist medicalised killing in Austria. In spring 1939 the Nazi regime implemented a euthanasia programme in Germany with the ostensible goal of restoring the 'racial integrity' of the German people and eliminating individuals deemed 'life unworthy of life' and, to that end, a clandestine operation was devised specifically to eliminate disabled children. Hitler authorised his personal physician Dr Karl Brandt and head of the Chancellery Philip Bouhler to introduce 'Children's Euthanasia'.[46] Remarkably, this was not introduced to apply solely to Jewish children, but to all children of the Reich, Germans included.

On 18 August 1939 the Reich Ministry of the Interior issued a decree mandating that all medical practitioners report newborns and children under the age of 3 years exhibiting severe physical or mental disabilities. Parents of such children were then approached and encouraged to bring their children to specialised paediatric clinics where they would receive appropriate care. However, the clinics were, in fact, death wards, the 'appropriate care' meant no care at all. Specially recruited medical staff at a number of selected locations were employed to murder these children

---

45 Documentation Centre of Austrian Resistance, ://www.doew.at (Weisz Oskar)

46 United States Holocaust Memorial Museum; https://encyclopedia.ushmm.org/content/en/article/euthanasia-program

through drug overdose or starvation. Between 1940 and 1945 some 800 sick or disabled children were murdered this way at Vienna's Steinhof Hospital. Earlier, in July 1939, with the murder of disabled children under way, Hitler approached Brandt and Bouhler again and asked that they develop a similar scheme to be applied to adult patients. In order to provide some level of legal cover for this extension of his Nazi racial 'enhancement', Hitler provided a written authorisation for Brandt and Bouhler to commit what was, effectively, mass murder. The original document was destroyed but a facsimile, made at the time and handed to the Reich Justice Minister Franz Guertner by Bouhler to prove that the direction actually came from Adolf Hitler, survives and is held today in the United States Holocaust Memorial Museum, on behalf of the US National Archives and Records Administration. A translation of this macabre document reads as follows:[47]

> Berlin, 1.Sept.1939
>
> Reichsleiter Bouhler and Dr Brandt, MD are charged with the responsibility of enlarging the authority of certain physicians to be designated by name in such a manner that persons who, according to human judgement are incurable can, upon a most careful diagnosis of their condition of sickness, be accorded a mercy death.
>
> (Signed). A Hitler

The instruction, although issued in October, had been back-dated to 1 September 1939, probably to cover potential war crimes that had occurred in the occupied Polish territories since

[47]United States Holocaust Memorial Museum; https://encyclopedia.ushmm.org/content/en/photo/adolf-hitlers-authorization-for-the-euthanasia-program-operation-t4-signed-in-october-1939-but-dated-september-1-1939

the outbreak of war when certain institutions were 'cleared' of patients to be used as barracks to house occupying soldiers.

A clandestine unit was established by Adolf Hitler to oversee the euthanasia operation, codenamed 'Aktion T4' (Operation T4). This codename was derived from a subtle reference to the Chancellery's address at Tiergartenstrasse 4 in Berlin.

In late 1939 the staff of Aktion T4 meticulously crafted a questionnaire to be distributed to health professionals responsible for nursing homes housing mentally and physically chronically ill patients. The pretence for this operation was to gather statistical information on patient numbers, relevant illnesses and, importantly, their potential work capacities. This data was not gathered for any medical purpose but to be used as intelligence to identify and mark patients for murder.

T4's medical staff reviewed the returned forms and compiled a selection list from each surveyed institution. From early 1940 T4 operatives visited those institutions and transported the selected patients by bus to one of six designated 'medical' centres equipped with gas chamber facilities. The facilities consisted of hermetically-sealed rooms into which carbon monoxide was introduced and released via valves and piped from bottled containers. The victims left within these rooms were killed within a matter of minutes.

In instances where gassing was deemed impractical, the victims were administered lethal doses of poison by medical staff. The exact number of individuals murdered in this manner remains uncertain, but it has been estimated to have been in the region of 70,000.

A separate Aktion T4 team at each location removed the bodies from the chambers and conducted on-site mass cremations. Relatives and loved ones of the deceased were subsequently provided with an urn containing ashes from the mass cremation, serving as a representation of their remains. Death certificates were issued indicating a falsified cause of death, typically pneumonia or pleurisy, far removed from the truth which was, of course, pre-meditated murder.[48]

On 18 November 1940 Rosalie Weiss was removed from her ward at the Am Steinhof Psychiatric Clinic in Vienna and transported by bus to the T4 facility in Hartheim near Linz. Upon her arrival, she was systematically murdered through gassing and her body cremated. An urn, purportedly containing her remains, was subsequently delivered to her husband, Oskar Weiss, and was interred by him in the Wiener Zentralfriedhof, Simmering cemetery, with a sickening irony, in section T4 or Tor 4, group 20, row 10, grave number 6. The burial ceremony took place on 16 December 1940. Less than three months later, on 5 March 1941, Oskar Weiss was forcibly deported from the holding centre at Kleine Sperlgasse 2a to Modliborzyce via Transport No.4, having been allocated passenger number 167.

Oskar Weiss had no incentive to remain in the open ghetto. At the age of 59, he made the decision to escape and departed from Modliborzyce on 16 September. He was never to return. The specific route he took and the assistance he received during his journey remain unknown. The distance to Vienna is substantial. By car today the journey would take approximately eight hours while, on foot, it is estimated to take close to two weeks, excluding the added dimension of possibly travelling at night to evade Einsatzgruppen and Gendarmerie patrols, with little food and no expectation of finding shelter.

What is certain is that Weiss managed to reach Vienna. This information is known solely because the details of his arrest were recorded in the Vienna Gestapo Daily Record Sheets (DRs) which were produced daily and highlighted significant occurrences from the previous twenty-four hours. The DRs were typically divided into sections covering subversive activity, searches, intelligence and arrests under the typical headings of

[48] Ibid.

socialism, Jewish activity, homosexuality and military desertion. An entry for 20 August 1942 translates as follows:[49]

> On the 20th August 1942 the Jew Oskar Israel Weiss 16.3.1882, born Sarajevo, was arrested without a fixed address.
>
> Weiss, who had been evacuated to the Generalgouvernement in August 1941, left his assigned place of residence without permission on September 16th 1941 and went to Vienna. He was transferred to the Jewish collection camp for evacuation.

The August 1941 date in the report is obviously incorrect since we know that Oskar was on board Transport No.4 in March of that year. Oskar survived for nearly a year after fleeing the ghetto before being apprehended by the Gestapo in Vienna. Clearly, he was unable to maintain a secure hiding place within the city and may even have been denounced. He was immediately transported to Auschwitz concentration camp where he was murdered on arrival on an unknown date in August 1942.

There is evidence of another attempt to escape the ghetto conditions at Modliborzyce, unfortunately also recorded in a Gestapo daily record report.[50] Max Steiner, a 54-year-old divorced typesetter, was forcibly deported on Transport No.4 on 5 March 1941 as passenger number 462. He had originally resided at Storkgasse 15 in the 5th District of Vienna and had moved to Vienna from Steinamanger in Hungary in 1906. Max secretly left Modliborzyce in May 1942 and made his way to Hungary. For months he remained at large, unable to find a permanent place to hide. He decided to make his way back to Vienna, arriving there

[49] Documentation Centre of Austrian Resistance, https://www.doew.at (Weisz Oskar)

[50] Documentation Centre of Austrian Resistance, https://www.doew.at (Steiner, Max)

in the middle of winter, on 23 December 1942. Once there, he managed to evade the authorities for only a few weeks until, on 6 January 1943, he was apprehended by the Gestapo. He was subsequently placed in 'protective custody' and imprisoned in Auschwitz concentration camp, after which there is no further record of his fate. It is widely believed that he was murdered at Auschwitz; his death was officially accepted for legal reasons in 1947.

At some point in December 1941 Ernestine Kessler and Helene König made their move to escape from Modliborzyce. We know little of the detail of the journey that lay before them other than a few lines from Helene, recounted some years later in two formal welfare application documents. In one she confirmed her friendship with Ernestine, initially meeting her at Kleine Sperlgasse in February 1941. She went on to describe leaving Modliborzyce:[51]

> After we decided to escape secretly from the ghetto due to beatings and hunger. I and Mrs Kessler managed to return to Vienna, on foot, at the end of 1941 after weeks of hardship.

She later gave a more detailed account of her escape from the ghetto, without mentioning Ernestine. The accounts originated from interviews conducted shortly after the war, when suspicions regarding the interviewers' intentions were still prevalent. Consequently, an element of caution was evident in the information imparted:

> People had to live in the most terrible conditions. After months of terrible suffering she [Helene] succeeded in fleeing from the ghetto and persuading a man to take her to the German border in a horse drawn cart. At the border this man took the few

[51] Documentation Centre of Austrian Resistance, document to author.

> possessions that she had from her. This was in December 1941. Under great hardship and physical strain Frau König succeeded in getting back to Vienna.

We know that the two women succeed in returning to Vienna, but the extent of the challenges they faced during their journey remains unknown, other than that they endured extreme weather conditions under the constant threat of encountering Nazi patrols or groups of partisans en route. As exemplified by the fates of Oskar Weiss and Max Steiner, reaching Vienna was a significant achievement, but survival in the city presented an entirely different set of obstacles. Their troubles were far from over.

***

By mid-1941 the Nazi Euthanasia Programme, initially a covert operation, had come to be an open secret among the German public, owing to the reporting of numerous instances of patient fatalities at specific institutions, all recorded with similar causes of death. The matter was highlighted by comments made publicly by the Catholic Church. Consequently, awkward questions were raised and protests were held demanding answers. As a result, Hitler closed down the operation for adults but continued with a programme of euthanasia for certain children in a more covert manner, which persisted until the end of the war. Although the T4 operation was shut down, the T4 administration staff were retained. In operating the first Nazi gas chambers, they had acquired the skills and the psychological capability to deliver the Final Solution.

On 31 July 1941 SS-General Reinhard Heydrich, chief of the Reich Security Main Office (RHSA) was directed by Reichsmarschall Hermann Göring to devise a scheme whereby the plan for the Final Solution, the deliberate, systematic mass murder of European Jews, would be drawn up and implemented across the Reich territories. On 15 January 1942 a conference of fifteen leading Nazi Party and government officials was held in a large villa in the Berlin suburb of Wannsee. The conference was convened by Reinhard Heydrich. Among those present were SS-Oberststurmbannführer Adolf Eichmann, now head of RSHA Department IV B 4 (Jewish Affairs) and the recently appointed State Secretary Dr Josef Bühler of the Generalgouvernment region or occupied Poland. The purpose of the conference was to allow Heydrich to inform the participants that he had been personally directed by Hitler to co-ordinate the operation and to secure support and compliance from the various officials present in its implementation. During the course of the meeting, Heydrich stated the following:[52]

> During the course of the Final Solution, the Jews will be deployed under appropriate supervision at a suitable form of labour deployment in the East. In large labour columns, separated by gender, able-bodied Jews will be brought to those regions to build roads, whereby a large number will doubtlessly be lost through natural reduction. Any final remnant that survives will doubtless consist of the elements most capable of resistance. They must be dealt with appropriately, since, representing the fruit of natural selection, they are to be regarded as the core of a new Jewish revival.

The European Jews were to be subjected to extreme labour, essentially worked to death, and/or murdered if deemed unfit. During the conference, Dr Josef Bühler presented a specific proposal, insisting that the Jews temporarily residing in the ghettos of the Generalgouvernment area be eliminated first. This

[52] United States Holocaust Memorial Museum https://encyclopedia.ushmm.org/content/en/article/wannsee-conference-and-the-final-solution

request was duly accepted. The scheme was designated with the code name Aktion Reinhard, honouring its RHSA head, Reinhard Heydrich. Lublin was chosen to serve as the operational headquarters for Aktion Reinhard, already the location of the SS-headquarters in the region. Odilo Globocnik, a close associate of Himmler, was appointed to oversee as the SS and Police Head of the Lublin district. With regard to the implementation of the scheme Heydrich had issued the following directive:

> In the implementation of the 'final solution', Europe will be systematically traversed from west to east. The evacuated Jews will be transported, group by group, to designated transit ghettos where, subsequently, the Jews will be relocated further east into the newly occupied territories.

Lublin's geographical location made it an ideal location for this purpose. If scrutinised regarding the disappearance of Jews from these ghettos, it could be argued that they were merely relocated 'further east' into the newly occupied Russian territories. Personnel tasked with the construction and operation of the death camps had to be sourced. The majority of staff were taken from the SS and police who were serving under Globocnik in the Lublin district and, most importantly, the existing Aktion T4 staff formed an important core of skilled staff, experienced in the euthanasia gassing operations.

In December 1941, as Ernestine Kessler and Helene König were making their perilous journey west towards Vienna, the first group of Aktion Reinhard personnel were heading east to Lublin to begin work in planning and carrying out mass murder. All of those involved were given SS rank, SS classification, and Waffen-SS field-grey uniforms and were led, notably, by Kriminalkommissar of Police Christian Wirth, appointed as SS-Haupsturmführer along with his adjutant SS-Oberscharführer Josef Oberhauser.

Wirth had come from a civilian police detective background and held a rank equivalent to a UK detective chief inspector, responsible for directing and carrying out investigations into serious crime in the Stuttgart area. Oberhauser had been a member of the SS-Leibstandarte Adolf Hitler battalion and had been stationed at Sachsenhausen concentration camp near Berlin in 1937 before being brought into the Aktion T4 euthanasia operation as part of the Reich Chancellery staff. During his attachment to T4, he was specifically employed as a *Leichenbrenner* or corpse burner at the crematorium ovens.

Straight away Wirth and Oberhauser set about seeking potential locations for three Aktion Reinhard extermination camps. Three camps were required, each to have access to the main railway network but to be out of sight from prying eyes. The camp sites selected were relatively small, roughly some 600-metres square, the reason being that those camps were death camps, set up for the murder, incineration and burial of remains of the Jewish ghetto occupants. There was no requirement for accommodation on site, save for that required to house guards and Jewish work parties or *Sonderkommando*. The three sites selected were Belzec, Sobibor and Treblinka which became known as the Aktion Reinhard death camps, constructed in the hinterland that existed in the wake of the advance of Operation Barbarossa, the Nazi invasion of the USSR.

Belzec was the first camp of the three to be built and became operational on 17 March 1942. It was very much a prototype camp and was used to bring together the elements learned in the Aktion T4 euthanasia programme and apply them to mass murder on a much larger scale.

Initially, the method of death applied was by using pure bottled carbon monoxide piped into three confined wooden sealed huts which gave the impression of being shower blocks. This process was soon disregarded as it entailed the supply and disposal of the gas bottles, therefore leaving an evidence trail and the possibility of detection along the supply route.. Since the camp had to be self-sufficient, the method of murder decided on was to be carbon monoxide poisoning, not from bottled gas but from the exhaust fumes of a captured Soviet 250-horsepower tank engine, initially piped into the three imitation shower buildings. As the months passed and demand increased, the three shower buildings were demolished and replaced with six concrete sealed buildings. No written orders were passed between those involved in the administration of Operation Reinhard, all orders being communicated verbally. Today there only exists written testimony from one person who survived being sent to Belzec camp. This testimony leaves us a valuable account of how murder was carried out on an industrial scale.

Rudolf Reder was transported to Belzec from the ghetto at Łódź in Poland on 10 August 1942.[53] Rudolf recalled that each transport was met by an SS officer who, in a calm and reassuring voice explained, 'You are going to bathe now, after that you will be sent to work.' Signs on display helped to further deceive the new arrivals into believing that they had arrived at a transit camp for work details displaying the instructions:

> Attention! Complete removal of clothing!
>
> All personal belongings, except money, jewellery, documents and certificates must be left on the ground. Money, jewellery and documents must be kept until being deposited at the window. Shoes must be collected and tied in pairs and put in the place indicated.

The station house, which was merely a facade at the arrival ramp and not a functioning railway building, was made up with timetables and posters, again to make the arrivals believe that they had stopped at a regular station, not a dead-end railway spur running alongside a death camp.

---

[53] https://www.jewishgen.org/yizkor/schindler/files/SchindlerAddendum.pdf Accessed 12/5/2025

On his first arrival at Belzec, Rudolf was beaten, dragged out of the main group and selected to become a worker at the site - in his own words, a member of the Sonderkommando, one of a group of 500 Jews who were temporarily kept alive by the Nazi guards to carry out the workings of the camp. These men, identified as being fit and relatively healthy when they arrived, were tasked with shaving the prisoners on arrival, removing their bodies from the gas chamber, digging burial bits to bury the bodies of those who had been gassed and then to cover the burial pits with sand and lime before the next transport arrived. Although slated for death, they remained alive until they were deemed unfit to continue the work whereupon they were shot and thrown into one of the pits that they had dug. Between forty and fifty Sonderkommando were murdered each day and replaced with newly-selected arrivals. Rudolf witnessed the processing of transport arrivals repeated day after day:

> Each transport received the same treatment. People were ordered to undress and to leave their belongings in the courtyard. Each time there was the same deceptive speech. And each time people rejoiced. I saw the spark of hope in their eyes – hope that they may be going to work. But a minute later, and with extreme brutality, babies were torn from their mothers, old and sick were thrown on stretchers, while men and little girls were driven with rifle-butts further on to a fenced path leading directly to the gas chambers. At the same time, and with the same brutality, the already naked women were ordered to the barracks, where they had their hair shaved. I knew exactly the moment when they all suddenly realised what was in store. Cries of fear and anguish, terrible moans, mingled with the music played by the orchestra. Hustled along and wounded by bayonets, first the men were made to run to the

> gas chambers. The guards counted 750 people to each chamber. Before all six chambers were filled to capacity, those in the first had already been suffering for nearly two hours. It was only when all six chambers were packed with people, when the doors were locked into position, that the engine was set in motion.

Rudolf Reder managed to survive at Belzec for almost three months until one day he was ordered by a guard to travel to Lviv to assist in carrying a load of metal sheets required for repairs in the camp. He was escorted by four Gestapo and one Ukrainian guard. After working all day moving the steel, he was left under the watch of one guard who eventually fell asleep. Rudolf seized the opportunity to escape, using his knowledge of the town to go into hiding where he remained undetected until he was liberated by the Russian army years later.

Following the successful operation of Belzec, the system of mass murder was replicated in the other two Aktion Reinhard death camps, Treblinka and Sobibor.

Leopold Kessler, Dr Paul Messinger and his wife Erna remained in the ghetto at Modliborzyce throughout 1942 under increasingly worsening conditions. By then, the Nazis had imposed a general curfew around the village: anyone caught outside the settlement limits would be shot on sight. Then, on 19 October 1942, the ghetto was sealed and the occupants were forced out of their accommodation. Those too ill to be moved or too old or frail to move fast enough were shot where they were. The remainder were gathered together and taken to the railway station at Zaklikow where a holding compound had been built. From there, trains were loaded, with 100 people crammed into each cattle car and they were sent further east.

Modliborzyce had become part of Aktion Reinhard. In reality, the village always had been in effect a holding camp, as arguably the 999 people sent there and added to the original Jewish population were never meant to survive. The means to murder them had just not been established until Belzec had been constructed. At Zaklikow Paul Messinger and his wife were separated from Leopold; up to that point they were both working as part of the Judenrat which gave some temporary benefits, which for Leopold ended then and there. Leopold was loaded into a cattle truck, part of a train which departed in an easterly direction with the remaining Jews from Modliborzyce. Paul Messinger, as a doctor, was put on a separate train travelling westwards. He recalled, however, seeing that Leopold Kessler was forced onto a transport train which he later discovered may have been destined for the death camp at Treblinka.[54] We now know, based on the times during which the three Aktion Reinhard camps were either operational or closed for modification, that the destination of that train at that time had to have been Belzec. We don't know the exact date, but on a date close to the end of October 1942, Leopold was forced off the train onto the ramp at the siding at the fake railway station at Belzec and, within two hours of arriving there, was murdered, one of thousands who suffered a similar fate.

***

Five months prior, on 27 May 1942, two Czech resistance operatives, Jozef Gabčik and Jan Kubiš, specially trained by the British Special Operations Executive, carried out an undercover operation in Prague against Reichsprotektor (governor) Reinhard Heydrich. Codenamed Operation Anthropoid, it was successful in that Heydrich was mortally wounded when an explosive device was thrown and detonated at the side of his staff car as it slowed down to negotiate a road junction in the city. The subsequent infection of his wounds led to his death in hospital just over a week later in the early hours of 4 June 1942. Reprisals, on a

[54] Documentation Centre of Austrian Resistance, copy document to author.

horrific scale, ordered directly by Hitler, led to the murder of an estimated 5,000 people.

In June 1943, following the exhumation and cremation of all bodies at Belzec extermination camp under the orders of Odlio Globocnik, the camp was liquidated. All the site structures were dismantled and the area was ploughed over. A manor house was constructed at the camp's edge and four-year-old trees were replanted in the area to create the illusion that the site had once been a farm. Those measures were undertaken in an attempt to conceal any evidence of the site's true purpose, that of the scene of the brutal robbery and mass murder of at least 434,508 people between 17 March 1942 and December 1942.

A specific number can be applied in the last paragraph owing to the discovery and analysis of two important documents which provided corroborated figures of the Aktion Reinhard operation. The documents were declassified for public release at the National Archives at Kew in the late 1990s and are referred to as the Hölfe message and the Korherr report.[55] The Hölfe message comprised two radio messages sent within five minutes of each other which were intercepted and deciphered by a British Intelligence listening post. The messages were sent and intercepted on 11 January 1943, the first at 1000 hours and the second at 1005 hours. Both messages were sent under the classification 'State Secret!', with the first addressed to the 'Reich Main Security Office, for the attention of SS-Obersturmbannführer EICHMANN, Berlin'. The remainder of the message was not received. The second message, however, sent under the same classification level gives an indication that it may have been identical to the first, sent to a different recipient, 'Senior Commander of the Security Police [and the Security Service], for the attention of SS-Obersturmbannführer HEIM, CRACOW'. Both messages were sent and signed off by 'SS and Police Leader Lublin, HÖLFE, Sturmbannführer'.

[55]https://www.nationalarchives.gov.uk/education/resources/holocaust/hoefle-telegram/

SS-Sturmbannführer Hermann Hölfe was a leading staff member subordinate to SS-Gruppenführer und Generalleutnant der Waffen-SS Odilo Globocnik in Lublin who held the specific title 'Section Head for Jewish Affairs – Aktion Reinhard'. The addressee of the message, 'HEIM', Franz Heim, was, at that time, the deputy of the Commander of the Security Police and SD for the Generalgouvernment region. The body of the message read as follows:

> Subject: Fortnightly report Einzatz REINHART
>
> Reference. Radio telegram therefrom
> Recorded arrivals until December 31, 42.
> L [Lublin] 12 761
> B [Belzec] 0
> S [Sobibor] 515
> T [Treblinka] 10 335
> Together. 23 611
> Sum total [as per] December 31, 42
> L. 24 733
> B. 434 508
> S. 101 370
> T. 713 555
> Together 1 274 166

At the time the message was intercepted the British Intelligence operatives had no idea of the significance of what they had received. The inclusion of 'L' for Lublin in the message is still unclear but recent research indicates that this refers to the Majdanek camp at Lublin which may have come under the scope of Aktion Reinhard during the final stages of the operation. In the original decipher the final 5 of the Treblinka figure 713555 had been dropped, reading 71355; an addition of the remaining figures with the 5 included gives us the identical final resulting figure of 1,274166. The spelling of the operation name 'Reinhart' can be attributed to a phonetic error by the signal operator or by a misunderstanding of the actual spelling of Heydrich's name; he had used the spellings Reinhard and Reinhardt in previous documents on different occasions over a period of years.

A corroborating document, tellingly titled 'Final Solution of the European Jewish Problem' was prepared by statistician Dr Richard Korherr and sent to Himmler's office, for the attention of Hitler on 23 March 1943.[56] Korherr was brought in to prepare the report after a previously prepared report on the subject, which was found to be unacceptable and rejected, had been prepared by Adolf Eichmann. Korherr's report was returned in order to change incriminating phraseology to indicate that Jews 'passed through' camps to the 'Russian east'. Unfortunately, Korherr's original terminology no longer exists but the relevant section of the report, under section 4 of his document states:

> 4. Transportation of Jews from the Eastern Provinces to the Russian East Number of those who passed. 1,449,693.
> Through the camps in the General Government. 1,274,166
> Through the camps at Warthegau. 145,301.

The Warthegau region mentioned in the report relates to Chelmno, not an Aktion Reinhard location, but a death camp all the same. It can be seen that the figure used in the Korherr document for those murdered in the Generalgourvenment is identical to that intercepted in the Hölfe signal. Analysis of both documents tells us that that the aim of the Final Solution was the transportation and murder of the Jews of Europe and to that end Aktion Reinhard accounted for at least 1,274,166 individual murders, with at least 434,508 of those committed at Belzec.

---

[56] Richard Korherr report; https://holocaustresearchproject.net/holoprelude/korherr.html, Accessed 12/5/2025.

Unknown to his wife Ernestine at that time and indeed for years to come, included among those crimes was the cold-blooded, premeditated murder of Leopold Kessler along with the remaining passengers of the original Transport No.4.

CHAPTER 6

"Aktion 12"- Resistance

Five days after the Anschluss on 18 March 1938, the Austrian Federal Railways Company, the BBÖ, was taken over by the German Deutsche Reichsbahn (DRB). This process, which took nearly a year to complete, resulted in the control by the Nazi regime of approximately 5,900 kilometres of operating track length, 2,122 locomotives, almost 39,000 passenger and freight cars and 57,000 employees.[57]

Many original BBÖ employees were dismissed due to their non-compliance with the Nuremberg Laws, particularly as railway workers were considered civil servants of the Reich. Additionally, employees involved in trade union activities and those who

---

[57] 'Verdrängte Jahre Bahn und Nationalsozialismus in Österreich 1938-1945' Projektleitung und Text: Dr inTraude Kogoj Wissenschaftliche Beratung: Univ.-Prof. Dr Oliver Rathkolb Eine Dokumentation, herausgegeben von der ÖBB-Holding AG.

adopted a more militant stance, including active socialists or communists, were also dismissed. Notably, those individuals who participated in the February uprising of 1934 took advantage of the situation to flee, primarily to Czechoslovakia. From 1939 onwards the workforce was increased to almost 105,000 employees, comprising both civil servants and railway workers, each one required to swear allegiance to the Führer.

Following the outbreak of war in September 1939, and particularly after the Nazi invasion of Russia in 1941, the demands on the railway system increased significantly. Trains played a crucial role in supporting troop movements and transporting supplies to the Eastern Front. Additionally, they facilitated troop rotations by bringing soldiers back from the front lines. The railways also experienced a substantial increase in freight traffic as the production of war materials, weapons and machinery surged. Notably, the railways played a pivotal role in the persecution and murder of the Jewish people and others forcibly transported by train to numerous work and death camps. Those camps were strategically situated at the termini of constructed rail spurs or within a short distance of the railway lines.

The existing, numbered forced deportation lists preserved in archives today serve as tangible evidence of the railways' dual purpose: facilitating the transportation of victims and, in effect, the robbery of the Jewish people through the process. These lists, compiled by Deutsche Reichsbahn, were employed to calculate fares for each journey, including those to ghettos and concentration camps. Subsequently, payment was sought and received from the funds of the Jewish Council, the IKG.

It is not surprising that the construction of a specific war locomotive was commissioned due to the immense importance attached to railways. This freight locomotive, designated the Class 52 Kriegslokomotive, was manufactured simultaneously at sixteen rail engineering factory sites across the Reich, including the

Henschel Group's Vienna Locomotive Factory Floridsdorf, situated in the north-eastern 21st district of Vienna.[58]

Consequently, the Class 52 locomotive was classified as a military product, effectively serving as a weapon of war. Along with this military classification came severe penalties for any individual who attempted to interfere with the production or operation of such a machine. As Vienna became a prominent transportation hub in the Ostmark region of the Reich, it facilitated rail deportations from the repurposed Aspang station, along with freight, military and civilian rail traffic originating from three substantial railway stations alongside the extensive Floridsdorf and Simmering railway workshops. Thus, the city presented a target-rich environment for individuals inclined to engage in sabotage of the railway infrastructure.

A family group photograph, in all likelihood taken by the Schrekinger family friend, photographer Karl Piekarowitz in 1916, shows Ernestine Kessler's family at the time when she was a young girl of around 14 years old, six years before she married Leopold.[59] The photograph captures a fleeting moment in time, presenting a family group of the five Schrekinger sisters, along with two boyfriends. Ernestine stands alongside her sisters Eleonore, Rosa, Berta and Anna whom Gertrude later recalled as the aunt who frequently babysat her and her younger brother Fritz. Remarkably, this photograph survives today solely because, several years after its capture, Ernestine concealed it within the small cardboard suitcase that she entrusted to her daughter during her evacuation from Vienna via the *Kindertransport* train.

Intended as a poignant reminder to a young girl of a family left behind in Vienna, the photograph serves as a tangible representation of the absence of her parents. In the absence of their physical presence, it provides a paper-based connection to her heritage and the lives of those depicted. Through the image, Ernestine intended to instil a sense of belonging and share

[58] Ibid.

[59] Warmington family collection.

cherished memories while imparting valuable lessons about her family's history, personalities, achievements and shared experiences. Under normal circumstances the mother would have leant over her daughter's shoulder, pointing to and recounting stories of those photographed intending to ground her existence, provide a framework for understanding her roots and potentially guide her own aspirations and goals. Today, the photograph retains no background information except for the first names of the individuals in the group which Gertrude has written on the back in pencil. This group photograph, however, when forensically examined alongside other documents held by the Warmington/Kessler family, unlocks a historically important narrative of courage and resistance against oppression. In a sense, the photograph symbolises the triumph of good over evil and highlights the fragile balance between the two.

Two young men in military uniforms are visible at the rear of group in the family photograph. The individual on the left has been identified as Josef Brenner while on the right beside him is Anton Vogelsang.

Josef Brenner was born in Vienna on 26 January 1898. Anton Vogelsang was born on 14 December 1898 in Judenburg, approximately eighty miles southwest of Vienna in the Styria district. From the age of 16 years Anton was employed by the Austrian Railways (BBÖ), breaking from this employment only to serve with Josef Brenner in the Austro-Hungarian army during the Great War. On the conclusion of hostilities, Anton Vogelsang relocated to Vienna and resumed his employment with the BBÖ. There he met and eventually married Eleonore Schrekinger. The couple had a son, also named Anton in 1921. Approximately ten years later, they moved into an apartment in the newly completed Red Vienna Karl Marx Hof complex in the 19th District, at Heligenstadter Strasse 84.

Josef Brenner later married and he and his wife Marie had a son, also named Josef, in 1924. The family settled in an apartment at Springergasse 14 in the 2nd District. Throughout their lives, the two men maintained a strong friendship and made similar work and life decisions. Josef Brenner took up a position as a material officer at the BBÖ Floridsdorf workshop complex while Anton Vogelsang was employed by the BBÖ as an inspection mechanic and, later, having completed the necessary examinations in 1925, was appointed wagon-master at the Franz Josefs station in Vienna.

Both men became activists in the trade union movement affiliated with the substantial railway workforce at the time under the leadership of the Social Democratic Party. As the years progressed, they increasingly shifted their support towards the Austrian Communist Party or Kommunistische Partei Österreichs (KPÖ).

In 1933 the KPÖ was outlawed by the Dollfuss Austrofascist government, which, following the coup of 5 March that year, compelled the organisation underground amidst a backdrop of continued suppression of workers' rights, wage reductions, employment benefits' curtailments and freedom of press and assembly restrictions. The government's policies eventually precipitated a general strike and civil war which broke out on 12 February 1934.

Violent clashes erupted in numerous Red Vienna social housing complexes, particularly Karl Marx Hof, which transformed into an urban warfare battlefield where government forces employed artillery against communist fighters who had fortified themselves within the area. Anton Vogelsang and Josef Brenner, both with prior military training and experience, found themselves engaged in a conflict that they had envisioned as a revolution, but which ultimately turned into a swiftly and violently suppressed uprising. On 12 March both Anton Vogelsang and Josef Brenner were arrested for their part in the uprising and detained. Brenner was imprisoned for six months in the police prison at Elizabethpromenade in Vienna, nicknamed *the Liesl*, known today as the Rossauer Lände, while Vogelsang was incarcerated for a year in the prison at Vienna Court No.2.

Both men were later released without trial due to the absence of any evidence against them.

Following their release from detention, the two men resumed their involvement in underground Communist Party activities and returned to work at the BBÖ where they played a pivotal role in establishing railway communist party cells *(KP-Gruppe)* at all major railway locations, thereby establishing connections with the main KPÖ leadership.

Following the Anschluss in March 1938, Anton Vogelsang, Josef Brenner and their comrades within the KPÖ and socialist underground found themselves under a new jurisdiction as they became highly sought targets of the Gestapo. This marked a significant shift in their status from being outlawed political activists to that of active resistance fighters. The Reichsbahn KP-Gruppe, as the Vienna Gestapo referred to them, was ideally positioned to disrupt the Nazi war machine with opportunities for sabotage throughout the railway network. Consequently, the likelihood of capture increased and the penalties were undoubtedly severe.

The Vienna Gestapo had the advantage as, on taking over the original Austrian Police structures, they inherited the various intelligence card indices and files on the socialist and communist enemies of the previous Austrofascist government. Those enemies conveniently became enemies of the Nazi regime. As a result, Anton Vogelsang was forced to retire from the BBÖ on 31 January 1939 under newly imposed regulations governing the salary structure of civil service employees and the restructured railway under the name of the Deutsche Reichsbahn. He was then arrested on 26 October 1939 and detained until July 1940 under the provisions of 'protective custody', most likely as a result of information relating to his KPÖ activities being uncovered by Gestapo investigators.

On release, as a retired railway worker, he continued with his KPÖ activities as leader of a KP-Gruppe cell at Franz Josefs station and as a cashier for funds gathered by the organisation at that location, funds used to support families of arrested communist activists under the name of "Red Aid".

At this time the Vienna Gestapo were already in advanced stages of infiltration of the KPÖ.[60] From the outset they employed intelligence gathering and surveillance tactics against the organisation with the tactic of 'enhanced interrogation', essentially brutal torture and beatings used as a means to 'turn' a suspect into becoming an informant, reporting on KPÖ cells or, ideally, an agent operating within the centralised higher structure of the organisation, essentially directing from within as an agent provocateur on the orders of Gestapo handlers. At lower levels the Gestapo used 'cell spies', prisoners who had previously been detained and turned, then offered an incentive, usually a stay of execution, to remain within the detention cells of the Gestapo and police holding centres where newly arrested prisoners would then be introduced to their cells to be greeted by a seemingly friendly face and begin talking freely. As a result, and with the powers available to the Gestapo to arrest almost at will, the KPÖ in Vienna began to be taken down at an alarming rate. A later report on the success rate of the Vienna Gestapo, dated 23 March 1944 gave a breakdown on arrests for the previous years; 742 arrests in 1938, 1,132 in 1939, 837 in 1940, 1,507in 1941, 881 in 1942, and for 1943 the figure was 1,173, a total for the period of 6,272 arrests. Out of these numbers 293 people were sentenced to death directly by the People's Court in Vienna.[61]

It is difficult to comprehend how, against such attrition, an underground organisation could continue to exist or, for that matter, how its members could continue to operate under the constant stress of threat of arrest and likely death, either by death sentence or 'protective custody' which by that time meant the high likelihood of a slow demise in a concentration camp.

---

60 *The Vienna Gestapo, 1938-1945 Crimes, Perpetrators, Victims*, Elisabeth Boeckl-Klamper, Thomas Mang, Wolfgang Neugebauer, Berghahn Books, New York, ISBN 978-1-80073-260-5.

61 Ibid.

The Gestapo daily record sheets give an indication of the levels of sabotage carried out, particularly across the railways. Predominantly, incidences of communist leaflets and flyers being printed and left in prominent locations are reported. Typewriters became an unexpected weapon of war with one report of a plainclothes Gestapo officer reporting hearing the sound of a typewriter in use coming from a railway office in the middle of the night. The KPÖ were involved in actions more directly related to the workings of the railway. By the end of 1940 the Reich Security Main Office (RHSA) reported that they were focusing attention on the activities of KPÖ operatives carrying out acts of sabotage on the railway network in the Carinthia and Styria regions as well as the Vienna city area.[62] The report cited the KPÖ as responsible for approximately forty-seven arson and bomb attacks since 1939. In addition, attacks on railway infrastructure included the cutting of brake coupling hoses, mixing sand with grease used to lubricate axle bearings on wagons, switching goods wagon markings to ensure incorrect destinations and making false telephone calls and telegrams redirecting entire trains. Each of these activities resulted in the most severe penalties when tried at the Vienna People's Court as offences of high treason or of undermining military morale. Conviction carried the prospect of death or, at the very least, deportation under 'protective custody' and detention in a concentration camp.

Despite these severe consequences, the resistance fighters persistently continued their activities in defiance of the Nazi regime. It is noteworthy that those individuals represented a substantial portion of the Austrian public, particularly in Vienna, who refused to accept the oppressive regime's actions. The figure of 6,272 arrests carried out in Vienna alone before 1943 serves as a testament to their unwavering spirit of resistance against tremendous odds. The resistance, however, with the exception of

---

[62] *Österreichs Eisenbahner im Widerstand,* Edited by Friedrich Vogl, 1968 Dokumentationsarchiv Des Österreichischen Widerstandes.

the assassination of Reinhard Heydrich in Prague, instigated and carried out by SOE operatives as a military operation, was restricted to sabotage. None of the Viennese resistance groups ever developed the resources or military capability to mount offensive attacks against the occupying Nazi forces. With the draconian powers made available to Gestapo investigators, combined with the network of informants, agents and denunciations by members of the complying public, the KPÖ eventually became infiltrated and fragmented, almost to extinction.

In January 1941 the Reich Security Service (RSHA) initiated an extensive investigation into Reichsbahn employees involved in the KPÖ. The enquiries revealed a connection between communist Reichsbahn customs officials in the Lower Danube region and employees operating KPÖ cells composed of Reichsbahn workers in Vienna and the St Polten areas.

Specifically, the Gestapo focused on an independent communist party group or *Reichsbahn KP-Gruppe* with cells operating within Vienna railway stations and the railway repair shops at Floridsdorf and Simmering. Those facilities were responsible for collecting and distributing funds for the Red Aid organisation.

By the late autumn of 1941 sufficient intelligence had been accumulated to identify the leaders and key figures of the Reichsbahn KP-Gruppe, enabling the formulation of an operation against them. The operation was codenamed 'Aktion 12', which referred to the twelve primary subjects under investigation, all of whom were railway workers.[63] They were:

1. Friedrich ZWICKL, born 27.1.1906, originally from Vordenberg, living in Vienna.
2. Mathias NAGEL, born 21.11.1899 from Vienna.

[63] Landesarchiv Berlin https://www.landesarchiv-berlin.findbuch.net 'Proceedings against Dr Emil Berndorff and others for the Special Treatment of Foreign Workers and Prisoners of War.'

3. Franz REINELT, born 27.6.1900 from Vienna.
4. Anton VOGELSANG, born 14.12.1898 from Judenburg, living in Vienna.
5. Josef BRENNER, born 26.1.98 from Vienna.
6. Otto WEHOFSCHITZ, born 20.5.1912 from Vienna.
7. Siegfried HARTMANN, born 27.5.1900 from Vienna, living at Bruck an der Leitha.
8. Leopold BAUER, born 21.9.1893 from Klosterneuburg, living in Vienna.
9. Robert SCHÖN, born 2.8.1882 from Vienna.
10. Anna ZWICKL née Bohl, born 9.9.1908, wife of Fredrich Zwickl.
11. Teresia MATSCH, born 18.9.1903 from Vienna.
12. Marie BRENNER, née Munduch, born 10.9.1899, living in Vienna.

The executive action taken relating to 'Action 12' was concluded over a three-week period commencing on 12 October 1941 with the planning and implementation of arrest and search operations against the twelve identified subjects.

Friedrich Zwickl, a railway conductor on the eastern line, and his wife, Anna, were the first to be arrested. They were taken from their residence at Hohlweggasse 21 in Vienna's 3rd district for interrogation at the Hotel Metropole Gestapo headquarters located at Morzinplatz 4. There was a protracted delay before the remaining arrests were made, starting on 1 December. The Zwickl couple were subjected to the intensified interrogation techniques employed by the Gestapo, one tactic being the torture of a family member in earshot or viewed through a cell peephole by the other party; the couple were prime candidates for this treatment. After weeks of torture and denial, Friedrich Zwickl finally 'broke' during interview and provided his interrogators with a confession. The inevitable wave of arrests followed.

Following the arrests, carried out on almost a daily basis, it became evident that the Gestapo had identified Mathias Nagel and Franz Reinelt as the group leaders. Nagel had previously been a train conductor on the Northern Line of the Vienna railway system. He had been involved in socialist activities since 1934 and, like Anton Vogelsang and Josef Brenner, had previously been detained – in his case in 1938 on suspicion of distributing propaganda newsletters along the railway route. Despite being imprisoned for several months, no offence was ever proven against him and he was later released and returned to his work at the railway. During 1940 Nagel became involved in organising clandestine meetings, including one in Salzburg that was attended by twenty people, with the intention of establishing additional KPÖ cells outside Vienna. Nagel's elevated profile had made him known to and reported on by the informants who had begun to infiltrate the KPÖ. As a result of the inevitable search of his home, the Gestapo recovered cash to the sum of 1,200 Reichsmarks, believed to be funds raised for 'Red Aid' purposes.[64]

On 2 December 1941 Franz Reinelt, a freight manager at the Matzleinsdorf station in Vienna's city centre, was arrested following a search of his home. Allegations against Reinelt included his involvement as a cash controller for the Reichsbahn KP-Gruppe and his role as a liaison officer at a district committee level within the KPÖ organisation. During the search of his property, the Gestapo seized a substantial sum of money and a 6.35 calibre pistol. The specific make and model of the weapon remain unknown but a firearm of that calibre and era would have been a compact and easily concealed weapon.

By all accounts 'Aktion 12', from a Gestapo perspective, was a success. All twelve of the main suspects had been detained along with sums of cash and a weapon also recovered. The initial arrests inevitably led to the identification and capture of other KPÖ members and Reichsbahn KP-Gruppe activists. Among the further arrests was Eleonore Vogelsang, the wife of Anton

[64] Ibid.

Vogelsang, and Ernestine Kessler's sister who was detained on 7 December 1941 on suspicion of being involved in communist activity.

The subjects of 'Aktion 12' were reported to the investigating judge of the People's Court of Vienna on 18 December 1941 for offences of high treason and were remanded in custody to stand trial at a later date.

By 14 July 1942 a total of 100 prisoners, which included six of the 'Aktion 12' arrests, had been convicted for high treason during sittings of the People's Court at Vienna and sentenced to be detained in 'protective custody'. Their number included sixty-seven railway workers, all communist resistance members; the remaining thirty-three were made up of Polish and Soviet prisoners of war. The protective custody sentence was ordered to be served at the Mauthausen concentration camp. On boarding the train for Mauthausen at Vienna, six of the sixty-seven communist workers were singled out, handcuffed, isolated from their comrades and placed in a separate cell car. The six men were Anton Vogelsang, Josef Brenner, Friedrich Zwickl, Franz Reinelt, Otto Wehofschitz and Mathias Nagel. Three witnesses described what happened next; all three were part of the transport and were also railway workers who ultimately survived their detention. Two of the three, initially identified as Franz S. and Johan P., may be identical to two names on the transport list of detainees who are known to have survived, Vienna railway workers Franz Schindl and Johann Piffl. On a date unknown they both signed the following joint statement:[65]

> On July 14, 1942, we, a group of 75 railway workers [author's note: sixty-seven railway workers appear on the original transport list], former members of the Christian-Social, Social Democratic and Communist parties, arrived at the Mauthausen

[65] 'Österreichs Eisenbahner im Widerstand'. Edited by Friedrich Vogl, 1968 Dokumentationsarchiv Des Österreichischen Widerstandes.

concentration camp at around 5 p.m. On the march from Mauthausen station to the camp gate, we could already guess what was to await us. Bumps with rifle butts, kicks and punches were dealt out by the SS escort indiscriminately and without the slightest provocation. Immediately to the right of the so-called Jourhaus (the SS gate house), we had to line up in front of the 'Wailing Wall' facing the laundry, where Bachmayer with his two Great Danes and several SS officers were stationed. Then they led the way. Before us, the camp commandant and the protective custody camp leader had let in our comrades, the 30-year-old ÖBB workshop worker from the Reichsbahn at Franz-Josefs-Bahnhof, Anton Vogelsang, the 42--ear-old freight calculator from the Simmering station improvement works, Otto Wehofschitz, the 44-year-old inspection fitter from Matzleinsdorf, Franz Reinelt, the 44 year-old material officer from the ÖBB workshop, Matthias Nagel, and the 38-year-old freight attendant from Floridsdorf, who was on duty on the Eastern Railway, Josef Brenner, and the 43-year-old leader Fritz Zwickl, who was employed on the Northern Railway. They were naked and their hands were tied. And then a so-and-so began. One after the other, the six who had evidently been chosen by the Gestapo as the most active members of our resistance organisation were called up and had to run about 100 metres between the laundry, the prisoner's kitchen and the perimeter guardhouse and at the same time two Great Danes belonging to the prison camp leader Bachmayer were set upon them. Our poor comrades, weakened by imprisonment and mistreatment, stumbled, fell and got up again while the Great Danes, trained to attack people, attacked them and inflicted terrible wounds.

> Otto Wehofschitz, who had to cover the distance twice, was the worst injured. Torn muscles and tendons hung from his arms and, covered in blood, he could hardly stand up. Comrade Vogelsang had his genitals bitten off and torn apart. We, who had to watch our colleagues being tortured as they screamed in pain and despair, were at the end of our strength. Some of us felt sick, vomited and soiled ourselves with our own excrement. After an endless 20 minutes, the six victims were led to the bunker. We were driven into the bathroom. The day after next, it was the 16th of September 1942, an SS commando escorted Wehofschitz, Vogelsang, Brenner, Nagel and Zwickl through the rear exit. A few minutes later, shots rang out and we knew that our friends had suffered. A handcart pulled by orderlies, covered with paper sacks, a bloody hand hanging down from the side, that was the last thing we saw of them.

This horrific account was corroborated by another witness, railway worker Leopold Mayer from Vienna, whose name also appears on the original Mauthausen transport list. He described the six men being singled out from the main group as above and then continued:[66]

> We lined up at the so-called 'Wailing Wall' in front of the prisoner bath. The six segregated prisoners stood naked behind the laundry. SS officer Bachmayer arrived with two dogs. He and other SS men insulted and beat the six 'ringleaders', forced them to run along the laundry and set the dogs on them. The trained dogs jumped on our comrades and tore off shreds of flesh and muscle up to shoulder height.

[66] KZ Mauthausen Memorial archives, Vienna; Account of Leopold Mayer, shelf mark V 3/32/2

> The horrific torture lasted about a quarter of an hour. Then the seriously injured were driven into the 'bunker'. We, the larger group, were taken to the bathroom. The showers were turned on as hot as possible and then we were immediately sprayed with cold water at full pressure from the fire hoses. The SS men were block leaders and members of the commandant's staff. Our entire group was also brutally mistreated. They also received blows with fists, ox-whips and beatings … .

Leopold Mayer's account was written and signed by him in Vienna on 7 August 1969. The six men, Anton Vogelsang, Josef Brenner, Friedrich Zwickl, Mathias Nagel, Franz Reinelt and Otto Wehofschitz, were not sentenced to death by the People's Court; instead, they were sentenced to be detained in protective custody. After sentencing, however, it appears that instructions were passed to the camp commandant at Mauthausen to implement 'special treatment', also referred to as 'special order no.8', for the six men. In effect, the six were not to be permitted to enter the camp population.

It is evident that the men were already singled out and isolated before leaving Vienna and placed in a cellular van, probably to facilitate a quick identification upon arrival at the camp, suggesting a level of premeditation at a high level regarding their eventual deaths.

The SS officer Bachmayer, whose name appears in both accounts, is identical to SS-Hauptsturmführer Georg Bachmayer, born on 12 August 1913. Bachmayer was responsible for protective custody prisoners upon their entry into the camp and gained notoriety for his brutal treatment of inmates. He, along with the camp commandant at the time, SS-Standartenführer Franz Ziereis, became known for their sadistic and brutal use of dogs to torture and murder prisoners: indeed, one dog was known to have answered to the name 'Lord'. Their method of torture was referred to among the inmates as 'Dying from the dog's kiss'.[67]

Entries were made in the arrivals' book at Mauthausen indicating that the six men did arrive, as stated, on 14 July 1942 and were allocated prisoner numbers from 11376 to 11381 inclusive. Further entries were made in a separate register of deaths recorded at Mauthausen Camp. For each of the six men, the entry recorded by the medical officer for the cause of death reads[68] 'Auf Befehl des Reichsführer-SS erschossen'. Translated as 'Shot on the orders of the Reichsführer-SS'. The date of entry is 16 July 1942. The Reichsführer-SS was, of course, Heinrich Himmler.

***

SS-Hauptsturmführer Dr Emil Berndorff was born in Berlin in 1892.[69] After completing elementary education, he pursued law and political sciences, graduating from the University of Berlin with a doctorate in law in 1920. Subsequently, he joined the Berlin police in 1921, assuming detective roles and becoming involved in investigations into serious crime. In 1933 he joined the Nazi Party and was appointed to the Secret State Police (Gestapo), where he handled Austria-related matters. Five years later he was promoted to the rank of SS-Hauptsturmführer and attached to Reinhard Heydrich's Reich Security Main Office (RSHA), where he headed Department IV C 2 (Protective Custody Matters). After the Second World War Berndorff went into hiding and assumed the identity of a farmworker near Husum in West Germany, a little

[67] International Military Tribunal, Nurnberg Germany, 13 December 1945, USA Exhibit 249.

[68] KZ Mauthausen Memorial archives, Vienna; Death register of the Mauthausen chief camp physician, shelf mark Y 46a.

[69] Landesarchiv Berlin https://www.landesarchiv-berlin.findbuch.net Proceedings against Dr Emil Berndorff and others for the Special Treatment of Foreign Workers and Prisoners of War.

village north of Hamburg close to the Danish border. In late 1945 he was discovered to be a Nazi in hiding and was subsequently arrested and charged with 'Belonging to a criminal organisation, namely the SS'. In 1947 he was sentenced to five years in prison and released in 1950, having previously served two years awaiting trial on remand.

On 26 June 1967 Berndorff was again arrested, along with eleven other former SS officers who had worked in the RSHA Department IV. He and his co-accused were charged with aiding and abetting the murder of 150 prisoners, all previously sentenced to protective custody but who had been identified by the RSHA office for 'special treatment', resulting in their executions. The names of those murdered in the 1941 Aktion 12 Gestapo operation were included as part of the 150 victims named in the investigation file against Berndorff and were specifically put to him during interview.

The prosecution against Berndorff and the eleven other co-accused was subsequently dropped due to a change in the law that related to prosecution time limits and maximum sentence lengths applicable to those charged with 'desk' offences, rather than those who physically perpetrated murders. Six months after his arrest, Emil Berndorff passed away on 1 January 1968, in Göttingen, Germany.

Of the remaining six Aktion 12 resistance fighters, little is known about their subsequent fate after their arrival at Mauthausen. Siegfried Hartmann was later transferred to Flossenbürg concentration camp and subsequently sent on to the Sachsenhausen camp, north of Berlin, where he is believed to have been executed. Leopold Bauer died less than two weeks after his arrival at Mauthausen, succumbing to exposure to continued brutal treatment. Robert Schön was transferred to Dachau concentration camp on 20 September 1942 and died there on 1 October 1942. His cause of death was recorded as 'circulatory disease and heart failure'.

No information is available to indicate how long Teresia Matsch spent in detention or where she was imprisoned. It is believed that she survived the war and continued to work for the Austrian Railways well into the 1960s at the Nordbahnhof station in Vienna.

Marie Brenner, the wife of Josef Brenner, a friend of the Schrekinger family, also survived her ordeal at the hands of the Gestapo. She continued to reside in Vienna after the city's liberation in 1945, accompanied by her son Josef and his wife Johanna. Marie Brenner passed away on 14 November 1989 at the age of 90 and is interred close to the graves and memorials dedicated to those who opposed fascism at the Friedhof Feuerhalle cemetery in Simmering, Vienna.

Eleonore Vogelsang was released from Gestapo detention on 23 September 1942. Detention photographs taken of her revealed evidence of mistreatment, including bruising around her right eye and left cheek.[70] On release she was required to report to the police station at Sickenberggasse 13 in the 19th District twice weekly on Mondays and Fridays. The bi-weekly reporting requirement would have had the effect of heightening any suspicions of her having been an informant as well as raising her own anxiety and fear of being returned to custody for interrogation each day she reported to the police. She likely experienced isolation within her community and, particularly, by members of the KPÖ. The reporting condition, in essence, was a Gestapo tactic to disrupt and sow mistrust.

In June 1946 Eleonore addressed her predicament in a letter, written by her to the Vienna State Railways, requesting a widow's pension. The report revealed that she had, by that time, gained

[70] Documentation Centre of Austrian Resistance, https://www.doew.at (Eleonore Vogelsang, née Schrekinger.)

knowledge of her husband's fate. An excerpt from her application reads as follows:[71]

> In December 1941 my husband and I were arrested and he was brutally murdered in Mauthausen on July 16 1942 as a political criminal. At the same time his pension was completely shut down.
>
> After my release from prison all my applications dated November 12th 1942 for approval of my legal entitlement to a pension, according to the decision dated January 18th 1943, sub E-pg 10-65772 u/N2, were brusquely rejected.
>
> Due to the denial of my pension I was placed in an extremely hopeless situation as I was completely penniless and received no family support.

Eleonore passed away in Vienna in 1974. Her remains were laid to rest in the Friedhof Feuerhalle cemetery at Simmering in Vienna.

On 16 July 1948, at the same cemetery in Vienna, just a couple of hundred metres from where Eleonore was later laid to rest, a memorial was built and remains to this day. The structure takes the form of two sets of three polished granite stones, each around a metre high, positioned left and right around a taller central stone. The three stones to the left of centre are inscribed with the names Fritz Zwickl, Franz Reinelt and Mathias Nagel. On the right, the stones bear the names Anton Vogelsang, Josef Brenner and Otto Wehofschitz. The six individual memorial stones mark the final burial locations of six urns containing the cremated remains of the six men which were recovered from a marked location at Mauthausen camp where they had been initially secretly buried by their comrades following their murders

---

[71] Landesarchiv Berlin https://www.landesarchiv-berlin.findbuch.net 'Proceedings against Dr Emil Berndorff and others for the Special Treatment of Foreign Workers and Prisoners of War.'

in July 1942. Their remains were exhumed from Mauthausen and reburied where they rest today on 20 July 1946.

The central stone is inscribed 'GEFALLEN IM KAMPFE GEGEN DEN FASCHISMUS KZ MAUTHAUSEN 16. JULI 1942'. Translated from German the inscription reads 'FALLEN IN THE FIGHT AGAINST FASCISM, MAUTHAUSEN CONCENTRATION CAMP, 16 JULY 1942.'

In the crisp autumnal sunlight in October 2024 Charlie Warmington and I walked toward the edge of a large circular section within the Friedhof Feuerhalle cemetery. The gravel pathway led us between cultivated hedgerows which opened up, inviting us to the entrance of a circular path. There before us was the memorial, made of two sets of three stones, one half matching the description given to Charlie by his mother years before. As Charlie stood in silence, absorbing the detail of the monument to his great uncle Anton Vogelsang, the family friend 'uncle' Josef Brenner and their four comrades, I looked on and recalled his chat from our first meeting:

> Two of my uncles were murdered by the Gestapo in Vienna for plotting to assassinate Adolf Hitler, they were killed by dogs … there are three stones somewhere in memory of them and another friend, I have no idea where.

The location of the memorial stones, tantalisingly described to him but never revealed by his mother, had been discovered. Along with them, the story of the six resistance fighters had come to light. Charlie realised that the blood coursing through his veins was not formed from the DNA of men who preferred to remain passive and indifferent, content to stand idly by and turn a blind eye as a murderous, oppressive regime overturned the world around them. As we stood back and absorbed the solemn scene, we noticed that a small wreath had been placed on Anton Vogelsang's memorial. Charlie then knelt down and examined a little lantern that was positioned on the ground beside it. He opened the glass door, and we could see that inside was a red candle, recently lit, its flame flickering in the breeze. Anton Vogelsang and the five other men were still being actively remembered by someone in Vienna, someone with whom our paths had almost converged.

***

If we acknowledge that the Nazi deportation of victims into deplorable conditions at Modliborzyce, where they confined the occupants of Transport No.4 to disease, starvation, overcrowding and exposure to extreme conditions was a deliberate method of murder then we must conclude that Paul Messinger and the other twenty-one doctors among their ranks were akin to resistance fighters. Indeed, the twenty-two physicians who had either been denied the right to practise among the general population or, in Paul's case, denied the opportunity to complete his final exams after completing his training, had lost one third of their number by the time the Modliborzyce ghetto was liquidated. His positioning as camp doctor attached to each of the work camps connected to Modliborzyce, at Lysakow and Janowska, undoubtedly contributed to his survival. Between 15 and 18 October 1942 the Nazi regime issued an order to liquidate the Jewish population held in ghettos within the Kleice-Janow region. To facilitate this directive, the ghetto at Modliborzyce was cleared and its inhabitants relocated to the railway town of Zaklikow.

Witness accounts indicate that SS-Einsatzgruppen, accompanied by Ukrainian auxiliaries, ordered the deportees into the town square. They subsequently identified and brutally murdered the sick, elderly and children as they stood there.

A subsequent selection process was conducted, involving approximately 500 Judenrat members, craftsmen and individuals in privileged positions, such as Paul Messinger, a doctor, who were all taken to one side. The remaining individuals were loaded onto railway carriages and taken to Belzec death camp for extermination. Those not selected were compelled to clear the town of the bodies of the deceased. Those were the circumstances in which Paul Messinger last saw Leopold Kessler alive. Paul remained at the rail camp at Zaklikow until 15 November 1942 when he was transported by train and interned in the concentration camp at Budzyń situated close to Lublin in occupied Poland.

By this time Paul Messinger had lost all his family with the exception of his brother Heinrich, whom he had previously assisted in emigrating to Uruguay. He had been separated from his 21-year-old wife Erna while they were incarcerated in the ghetto at Modliborzyce. He later discovered that Erna had been spared from being transported to Belzec but had been diverted to the Auschwitz concentration camp where she survived for two years until, in November 1944, she contracted tuberculosis and later succumbed to the disease in the camp hospital.

Paul's 57-year-old mother, Jetty Vermes, and his 11-year-old sister, Elisabeth, remained in their home at Neustiftgasse 93 in the 7th District of Vienna until 2 November 1941 when they were removed from the property and taken by train from Aspang station to the Łódź ghetto, renamed as Litzmannstadt by the Nazis. From that point their eventual fate is unclear. Paul later understood that they were murdered on being transported again to Auschwitz concentration camp in 1942. It is more likely, however, with the uncovering of more recent evidence, that they were murdered at Chelmno death camp, a prototype camp which was part of Operation Reinhard where the Nazis employed the use of gas vans to murder the inmates by re-routing the carbon monoxide exhaust fumes of the vehicle engine into a sealed rear compartment where the victims were held.

In spite of the whereabouts of his family being unknown to him from October 1942, Paul Messinger was resolute in his determination to survive. He recognised that by doing so and by using the medical knowledge he had acquired at the University of Vienna, coupled with his practical experience in applying those skills to mitigate the spread of disease within the ghetto, he was making a stand against the Nazis. He understood that each life he could save ultimately represented a victory over the regime and, for each of those lives, the potential for a future witness to testify to the atrocities inflicted upon the Jewish population of Europe. From that point forward, Paul Messinger engaged in what can be termed as medical resistance. Although he was unable to save the lives of the approximately 300 deportees who perished at Modliborzyce or the remaining survivors from Transport No. 4 who were murdered at Belzec, his subsequent efforts undoubtedly saved the lives of many individuals.

We are aware of these individuals now due to the existence of two handwritten testimonies, which Messinger wrote in Vienna on 19 January and 23 October 1945. Additionally, information provided by him in support of an emigration application to Israel made in 1950 contributed to this knowledge. These records were preserved by his son Daniel and were supplemented by information obtained through painful conversations he had with his father once Daniel grew to become aware of what his father had endured. Corroboration is available in the form of testimony from another doctor, Dr Friedrich Walter Forster, also from Vienna, passenger number 938 on Transport No.4 to Modliborzyce, and whose persecution for a period paralleled that of Paul Messinger which further substantiates the broad outline of Messinger's journey.

Paul was held at Budzyń, a forced labour camp for prisoners who worked at a nearby factory making components for Heinkel aircraft. Work first began at the factory at around the time of Paul Messinger's arrival there in November 1942, following a visit and inspection of the facilities by Ernst Heinkel in July 1942. An agreement was reached whereby Heinkel would pay 10 Zloty per day for each worker supplied from the concentration camp in order to feed the workforce. In reality this money was syphoned off by the SS, leaving very little with which to feed the inmates. As with other camps, to state that conditions were appalling is an understatement. The level of brutality and murder meted out was influenced by the personality and depravity of the camp commandant who, from early 1943, was SS-Oberscharführer Reinhold Feix. Feix came with a curriculum vitae which included the position of commandant at the Belzec death camp, having succeeded Christian Wirth. He was a man well used to mass murder.

In summer 1943 the Nazi Air Ministry directed that mass production of parts for the new Heinkel 219 twin-engine night-fighter would commence at the Budzyń plant. This effectively placed a higher economic value on the forced labour and contributed to the saving of the Budzyń camp at a time when all other nearby camps were being liquidated, at a loss of some 40,000 lives. Paul Messinger alluded to this event in his account dated 23rd October 1945:

> Again other camps, death camps, many die, dreadful conditions. I have many enemies, my life is threatened every day, hunger, lice, three dreadful months, I get very down, only one thing holds me up, hope. A sudden stroke of luck saves me. The prisoners are working for an aircraft factory (Heinkel).

Paul was quick to take advantage of the elevated status at the camp and using his initiative and somewhat protected status as a doctor he managed to position himself into a management role within the Jewish structure of the workforce:

> As a Jew I manage to find accommodation in an office. I prove myself well and get more and more orders and even as a prisoner I have such power that I become the construction manager's right-hand man. That is the most important position in the factory, in the end I have the overall organisation of

> the factory in my hand and rebuild it completely with Jews. (1½ years).

Paul set about to use his position and knowledge of the workforce labour requirement to re-position and select workers into more valuable positions. He also used his medical status as a camp doctor in declaring them fit to work when they otherwise might not have been, effectively saving lives. Disease was rife among the inmates, spread by the omnipresent lice; any prisoner deemed unfit for work was shot or transported for execution: 'I believe that several thousand Jews from this concentration camp remained alive because of this.'

Reinhold Feix's general treatment of Jews in the camp and specifically the sick is exemplified in the account of Paul Messinger's colleague at Budzyń, Dr Friedrich Forster:[72]

> A few days after he [Feix] arrived, he demanded that the camp inhabitants be paraded before him, and he sorted through them. Those people he sorted out he shot himself behind the barracks by shooting them in the neck. That was 97 people. In later action, he took once another 30, and once 28, and once 15 Jews, and apart from that, he also shot 5 people a day just for the hell of it. For each and every man who left the camp [escaped the camp] he would shoot ten other people [Jews]. Once, during a large flu and typhus epidemic, I had a large group of 260 sick people in the hospital. He wanted to shoot all 260 of them. Because of my energetic interference, he contented himself to shoot only 27 of them. They had to crawl on all fours to the final place where they were shot because they could not walk anymore. They had been beaten badly by the Ukrainian guards,

[72] United States Holocaust Memorial Museum: Dr Friedrich Walter Forster collection, Accession Number: 2007.313

> among others, with their guns and had been beaten down to the floor and could no longer get up.

The treatment of the sick by the camp doctors became a tense juggling act, played with the lives of the ill. The doctors had to time admissions and discharges from the camp hospital carefully; if Feix deemed anyone there unfit for work, they would be killed:

> Feix came to my clinic every few days and took patients who had lasted too long for him and took them away and shot them. Many whom I managed with much trouble to take care of and who were recuperating, lost their lives at this time.

Both doctors described how alongside their medical resistance efforts they became involved with sabotage at the factory works. Paul Messinger, with previous experience of sabotage in altering the transport plans while working at Operation Gildemeester in Vienna, did not let the chance of disruption at the Heinkel works go by. He simply wrote:

> No aircraft left from this factory. When it was finished we had to leave and the Russians took over a fully developed factory. (June 1944).

Friedrich Forster also recounted being involved in sabotage at the plant, perhaps more eloquently describing his deadly activities as follows:[73]

> practically nothing was produced in the factories because we had insufficient materials. What one hand built up the other hand destroyed it.

---

[73] Ibid.

In the face of the Red Army advance westwards following the failure of the Nazi Operation Barbarossa and subsequent offensive and, invariably, defensive operations on the Eastern Front, the facility at Budzyń was abandoned, leaving, as Paul described, a virtually intact factory in the hands of the Russians. Both Paul Messinger and Friedrich Forster were moved once again to another Heinkel factory situated some 150 metres deep underground in a repurposed salt mine at Wieliczka near Krakow. Again, Paul managed a failing factory, on this occasion for a period of only six weeks when once more the continued Russian advance forced the abandonment of the site.

On 27 May 1944 Paul Messinger was again forced into a crammed railway cattle truck and taken to yet another concentration camp. On this occasion his destination was Plaszow in the southern suburbs of Krakow, the city in which he was born. The camp at Plaszow had been constructed in 1942 as a work camp. By the time of Paul's arrival it had been filled to overcapacity and was operated as an extermination camp where the detainees were killed through excessive physical labour and regular shootings by the SS guards. In 1944 the work consisted of exhuming the thousands of buried bodies of previous murder victims and incinerating them. Once the work parties completed this task, they were in turn murdered to complete the eradication of evidence of mass murder.

During his detention at Plaszow, Paul engaged in a perilous dance, perpetually striving to maintain favour with the camp commandant, the notorious SS-Unterscharführer Amon Göth. Scant details of his experiences at Plaszow exist, possibly reflecting the harrowing nature of his relatively brief stay there. Paul recognised that survival depended on his proximity to Göth and described his experiences in general terms in his writings.

> I've seen thousands die, by bullet, by hanging, burning, hunger, torture, lice and other vermin and other things. Thinking about it brings me out in a

> sweat. I too have had a rifle at my chest and a revolver at my temples. That I'm still alive seems to me almost unreal.

When questioned about his time at Plaszow by his son Daniel, Paul made only one or two remarkable and chilling verbal comments which were passed on to the author in 2024, revealing the extent of his near-death experience at that point.

To ensure his survival, Paul cultivated a close relationship with Göth, leveraging his medical expertise and the knowledge gained from enduring four years of deplorable conditions within the concentration camps. He consistently drew upon his medical training and the moral principles associated with it, prioritising survival above all else and extending it to as many individuals as possible. To achieve this, Paul managed to gain Göth's trust as his private physician.

During this period, Paul discovered that Göth had a mistress residing in his quarters and who shared a particular fondness for piano music, particularly Ludwig Van Beethoven's 'Moonlight Sonata' in C sharp minor. Coincidentally, Paul Messinger possessed the knowledge and skill to play the piano, including 'Moonlight Sonata'. Göth's mistress repeatedly requested that he perform the piece for her, which ultimately saved Paul's life. Paul was kept alive in order to entertain.

Daniel shared another conversation with his father, which many readers can relate to. In reference to his father's line, 'I too have had a rifle at my chest and a revolver at my temples', Daniel enquired if I had seen the Steven Spielberg movie 'Schindler's List', based on the book *Schindler's Ark*, a historical fiction written by Thomas Keneally, based on true events and the activities of the industrialist Oscar Schindler, published in 1982. Naturally, I had. He directed me back to his father's written account, made in 1945 almost forty years previously, and stated, 'The scene from the film, "a revolver at my temples" that occurred to my father, he told me that he felt the click of the gun against his head, but it did not fire.' Indeed, there was a scene in the film where a pistol is placed to the head of a Jewish inmate and, on the pulling of the trigger it fails to fire, as does a second pistol. I vividly recalled the scene because it involved a continuity error. The actor, Ezra Dagan, playing the character Rabbi Levartow is confronted by Ralph Fiennes playing Amon Göth, who attempts to execute him with two semi-automatic pistols that both fail to fire. At the end of the scene, Göth is depicted walking away and throws the weapon down in disgust, at which point it can clearly be identified as a revolver, not the semi-automatic pistol depicted moments earlier in the scene. Daniel reiterated, 'That happened to my father.'

Daniel located survivors in Israel who had been acquainted with his father. Notably, those individuals had personally benefitted from his life-saving actions. Each survivor shared harrowing and tragic experiences, acknowledging that they had been compelled to transform into individuals they no longer recognised in order to endure. Regrettably, for every life saved, numerous others perished.

In the Plaszow camp, a prisoner was fortunate to survive for four weeks. Paul survived his harrowing encounter with death for six weeks before being transported once more. On 15 July 1944 he believed his luck had finally come to an end. The train onto which he was forced, after two days of travel, arrived at the now infamous railway ramp area of Auschwitz concentration camp. From his testimony, he wrote:

> Transportation to Bavaria, we go via Auschwitz and we believe that our last hour had come. But we go on, Flossenbürg concentration camp. After a week Leitmeritz concentration camp on the Elbe. The most dreadful conditions, many dead from the work and hunger. Every month about a third of the camp died. I stayed there 10 months. On April 24 1945, we are already reaching the new time, we are being

> transferred to Theresienstadt concentration camp, later I find out for extermination.

On 24 April 1945 Paul Messinger was transported in another cattle wagon to his eighth concentration camp, Theresienstadt.

CHAPTER 7

"U-Boote"- Proof Of Life

During the winter of 1942, Vienna experienced exceptionally frigid temperatures with January of that year recorded as being the coldest January ever documented in the city. The average daily high temperature reached only - 6.8°C, while the average low dropped to - 11.5°C. Amidst those unforgiving conditions, Ernestine Kessler and Helene König, still travelling together, arrived in Vienna on foot, concluding their arduous journey from Modliborzyce. Having endured robbery and physical hardship exacerbated by the extreme environmental conditions, Vienna offered little respite and presented the two women with only additional challenges, the most pressing being where to live without risking detection, arrest and deportation to a concentration camp. The only option open to them was to find someone who would be prepared to take them into their home and hide them, indefinitely.

This proposal entailed placing a potential host in a precarious position should new or unfamiliar occupants be detected at a property and reported to the Gestapo by unsympathetic neighbours. Practical challenges would need to be addressed, such as securing food during rationing for an additional person and providing adequate space within a property to accommodate safely an extra individual without detection. The majority of housing in Vienna at that time, as it is today, consisted of multi-storey apartment blocks that could be overlooked from the windows of neighbouring blocks and from opposite the ubiquitous courtyards behind. Wooden floors, increased noise, footsteps and even the use of toilet facilities all posed difficulties within the confined living spaces if an additional occupant was to be kept in a property undetected.

It seems that both women had thought of their own separate plans; without prior contact with their potential hosts the success of any such plan depended on what happened immediately after their door was knocked. The decision made by the occupant during that split second on opening a door really meant life or death for all concerned. In the case of Ernestine Kessler, it appears that her plan may have been formulated with the assistance of Leopold prior to her departure from the ghetto. The Kesslers were in possession of a piece of information that they had been aware of since January 1940. Although it may not have held significant value at the time, the circumstances surrounding it led them to formulate their plan.

Helene Piekarowitz, the wife of the photographer and family friend Karl Piekarowitz, had passed away on 21 January 1940 before Ernestine and Leopold were transported to Modliborzyce and some months after Gertrude and Fritz had had their Kindertransport photographs taken.

The Piekarowitzs resided as a couple in Vienna without any other family members. They occupied an apartment above Karl's photography studio at Rauscherstrasse 4 in the twentieth district. Helene Piekarowitz was 57 years old at the time of her death in

1941 while Karl was 61. The living quarters were situated directly above the photography shop and studio, which was accessible to customers from the street and, also, via a communal entrance and stairway.

Given the circumstances, including the layout of the premises and the recent passing of Helene, it appears to be an almost ideal location for concealing someone. There were no occupants living below the apartment, as the ground floor was the photographic studio, effectively minimising noise disturbances. Although the extent of awareness among neighbours regarding Helene Piekarowitz's passing remains uncertain, if Ernestine were to occupy the apartment and be observed through windows, she could be mistaken for Karl's wife. Furthermore, with the frequent comings and goings of customers through the premises, an unidentified woman could easily be passed off for a customer. The apartment also had the advantage of having two distinct entry and exit points, either via the communal stairwell or directly down the private staircase into the photographic studio below and out onto the street, potentially providing a means of escape should the need arise.

In any case, if Ernestine had attempted to seek refuge with her sisters she would have learned of the Gestapo's actions against Eleonore and Anton Vogelsang. She would also have learned that the Schrekinger family, with connections to the communist resistance, was either detained or likely to be under surveillance at that time. Ernestine had only one chance, and she chose to visit Rauscherstrasse 4, probably during Karl's studio opening hours when a stranger entering the premises could easily be mistaken for a customer. There, she approached Karl for assistance.

Karl was faced with an immediate decision: to welcome Ernestine into his home and commit himself to the constant strain of anticipating a knock on the door from the Gestapo, or to turn her away and continue his life. Karl understood that, by rejecting her, he was condemning her to death. Conversely, by bringing her in, there was a chance that both could survive or both would be apprehended, their fates becoming intertwined. It was evident that he was placed in an impossible situation. Ultimately, he chose to assist his family friend by bringing Ernestine into his home and concealing her within the property. Ernestine had become what was known as a *'U-boot'*, literally translated as 'U-boat', or submarine. She had effectively vanished beneath the surface of society and gone undercover.

Less is known about Ernestine's friend, Helene König, except that she had devised a similar plan for survival in Vienna. Helene reached out to an old acquaintance, comparable to Karl Piekarowitz, a non-Jew named Lucie Munk. Lucie, confronted with the same dilemma, admitted Helene into her home, an apartment located at Blaumergasse 24 in Vienna's 2nd District. In many respects, Lucie faced a more challenging task in concealing another person in her home. Her apartment lacked the space or luxury of having a connected business premises beneath it and she was known as a single woman living alone. Consequently, the two women would have to take the utmost precautions to remain undetected.

By the nature of their adopted *U-Boote* status in Vienna, from then onwards we know practically nothing of how both women and their hosts survived. No records were kept nor diaries recorded. Any records made would have provided incriminating evidence if they were detected. To venture outside into the city was too high risk to contemplate, although it is believed that of the recorded 600 or so cases of undetected *U-Boote* who survived, a few were forced into the open to attempt to obtain food on the black market, ration cards being unobtainable without identity documents.[74] In the case of Ernestine and Helene, it is evident that, by the time they had funded their escape from Modliborzyce and were robbed by the individual who had initially assisted them, they were probably destitute on arriving in Vienna. They were

[74] C. Gwyn Moser, 'Jewish U-Boote in Austria, 1938–1945', *Simon Wiesenthal Center Annual* 1985

certainly in no position to contribute financially to their own concealment. They relied solely on their hosts.

However, Ernestine harboured a singular, overriding desire. Since bidding farewell to her children in April 1939 her only contact with them during their stay at Millisle in County Down had been three brief telegrams, each consisting of twenty-five words, facilitated by the International Commission of the Red Cross (ICRC). Gertrude and Fritz had not received any communication from her or Leopold for over a year. Having endured the most arduous hardships, Ernestine felt compelled to re-assure her children of her survival and re-affirm the hope of their possible reunion. Her predicament was clear: how could an individual in hiding communicate with the outside world without jeopardising their safety?

Ernestine and Karl Piekarowitz ingeniously devised a remarkable scheme, the precise details of which remain undisclosed to this day, allowing her to communicate a message to her children indicating that she and Leopold were alive and well, despite the immense distance separating them. The scheme relied on Karl's photographic expertise and resources to fabricate a document that would persuade Gertrude and Fritz that everything was in order in Vienna when, in reality, that notion could not have been further from the truth.

The first stage in informing her children that all was well took the form of a photograph. Ernestine had Karl Piekarowitz take a studio photo-graph of her while she was in hiding at Rauscherstrasse. The idea of her doing this, without the assistance of Karl, at another Viennese photography studio would have been absurd and would most likely have led to her discovery when one considers the general conversation that would have taken place between the photographer and client during such a portrait session. Having to return at a later date to collect the final prints would have posed an extra danger in the process should any suspicion around Ernestine's status have been given away during the initial session, leading the photographer to tip off the Gestapo. By that time in Vienna no Jewish photographers were in business; indeed, with the continued timetable of deportations having taken place in her absence the entire Jewish population had been reduced to fewer than 10,000. Ernestine could eliminate those risks as she had the luxury of being able to go through the whole process, from the taking of the image to the developing and processing of the final print without her having to leave her safe hiding place.

The photograph was captured in a formal studio setting and printed onto a Kodak photographic postcard which was the customary practice during that era. The original photograph is still in existence and has been entrusted to Charlie among the other cherished documents and items left to him by his mother. On initial inspection, the photograph appears rather unremarkable. However, delving into the context of the image and deciphering the subtle message it was intended to convey to its 15- and 13-year-old recipients, we uncover its ingenuity and significance.

The image depicts Ernestine Kessler posed in a professional studio setting. Her right elbow rests on a tall plant stand against a backdrop depicting an elaborate classical garden scene, a hallmark of studio set-ups during the early twentieth century. Notably, Ernestine is portrayed without any make-up and is not wearing any visible jewellery, such as earrings or a necklace. Her hair is cut short and tucked beneath a small dark crocheted beret. She is wearing a dark coat with fur-lined cuffs and collar, with the sleeves perhaps just too short on her wrists; the length of the coat also falls just a few inches short of the dress that she is wearing beneath it. On her hands are dark velvet dress gloves and in her right hand she is clutching the handle of an elaborate handbag with a locking clasp. On her feet she is wearing what appear to be ankle-length winter zip-up boots.

In the photograph Ernestine is not smiling, she has a stern expression and is looking slightly to the right of the frame, as if she has caught the photographer's eye, left of camera, just as he took the shot, rather than looking into the lens of the camera beside him. A reflection of light can be seen in her eyes and on the clasp of the handbag she is holding which may indicate that the shot was taken with the use of a flashgun, perhaps supplementing light from a large window to the right of the camera, the resulting image being evenly exposed across her face and body with a slight fall-off of light behind her and to the left of the frame. The image has been printed full length, portrait style, head to toe onto the full length of the Kodak postcard and the card has at some point been folded to form a square, leaving a horizontal crease just below the centre of the subject.

When we consider the context of this photograph a number of points stand out. Ernestine's hair has been cropped short and to a greater degree is concealed by the hat she is wearing. In correspondence written from the Modliborzyce ghetto by Hermine Kubie to her son in Geneva, she informed him that she had cut her hair into a 'bob' style to keep the lice infestation at bay and it appears that Ernestine was forced to do the same thing. The lack of jewellery on show in the photograph nods to the fact that she had been robbed and indeed was forced to sell all she had to fund her journey back to Vienna. The wearing of gloves likewise covers the fact that her wedding ring and any other rings that she may have had were now gone, details that would have been noticed certainly by her daughter Gertrude, maybe not so much by Fritz when they looked at the photograph. Likewise, the expensive looking leather handbag held by her in the photograph and the fur-lined coat, which appears to be too small for her, would have been among the first items sold or exchanged at the ghetto for food. Finally, the boots she is wearing in the photograph appear to be spotless, certainly not worn in the muck and filth of Modliborzyce nor on the journey from there to Vienna during the depths of a hard winter.

Ernestine's general appearance in the photograph is not that of a lady attending a professional photographic portrait shoot, wearing outdoor clothes, coat, hat, gloves and boots, nor does it

depict a woman who has escaped from a ghetto. In reality, the clothes and handbag were likely those of Helene Piekarowitz, the recently deceased wife of the photographer. The photograph essentially is that of a woman making a defiant statement. At that point she had won a battle against the Nazis; she next had to survive the war.

Ernestine's expression appears weary yet resolute, akin to that of an endurance athlete posing for a photograph after conquering a formidable physical challenge, such as ascending a mountain or completing a marathon. At the time the photograph was captured, likely in February 1942, Ernestine could have been forgiven for feeling exhausted and emotionally distressed, yet strong and proud for having achieved her objective thus far, particularly preserving her life. This photograph stands as one of the most significant instances I have encountered of photography's ability to convey a message of hope amidst profound despair. Its true meaning was perhaps, and understandably, lost once it eventually found its way into the hands of its young recipients. Gertrude and Fritz just saw in the photo an image of their mother, safe and well, which was exactly what Ernestine intended. In the eighty years since it had been similarly regarded as 'just a photograph of Ernestine' by Charlie Warmington, his late brother Alan and the other family members who have viewed it; it is only now that the photograph can be seen for what it in fact was: it signified proof of life, a defiant message sent by Ernestine to shout out to her children that she was still alive and to instil in them the impression that all was normal. They weren't to know what she had been through, nor what lay ahead. Tellingly though, on the rear of the postcard Ernestine wrote the following message:

> Meinen lieben Kindern in herzlicher Liebe!
> Von eūrer Mūtti!
> Vater wollte nicht mitgehen sonst würde die platte springen!

The message, once translated reads,

> To my dear children with heartfelt love!
> From your mother!
> Father didn't want to go or the plate would crack!

She had made an excuse for Leopold not having been with her in the photograph and made an attempt to cover for his absence in the form of a joke – that his appearance would crack the photographic plate; an indication that Piekarowitz was still using large format glass plate negatives. She wanted the children to believe that they were living a normal life in Vienna and that both she and their father were still together. In reality, at the time the photograph was taken, Leopold was most likely working with Paul Messinger as part of the Judenrat at Janowska labour camp near Modliborzyce. In fact, Ernestine had really no idea if he was still there or even alive at all.

With the photograph taken, Ernestine had to figure a way of sending it to Millisle in Northern Ireland. The clue to how that was achieved also lies with the Warmington family.

Three letters remain with the family which were sent from Vienna to Northern Ireland. The first of the three was sent from Vienna to the Childhaven centre at Donaghadee in County Down on 26 April 1939.[75] It was sent via the Society of Friends at Singerstrasse in Vienna and served as an immediate reassuring follow-up letter, sent soon after Gertrude and Fritz's *Kindertransport* train departure. The address on the letter was written in as Streffleurgasse 4/41, the address to where the family had been moved following their eviction from their Leystrasse apartment. This communication, not a full letter, took the form of a short pro-forma allowing five lines of handwritten text to be included. Translated it read as follows:

[75] Warmington family collection.

> Dear Children, warmest kisses to you! You don't need to worry about us! We are healthy! Hopefully you are too. Are you still together in the home? Hopefully you are all well! So again: don't worry! 1000 kisses!

In contrast, one ICRC letter stands out as distinct from the others. The letter, dated 22 January 1942, was despatched by Ernestine Kessler and addressed to 'G&F' Kessler at Childhaven, Millisle Road, Donaghadee, Down, Northern Ireland.[76] The letter underwent processing at the ICRC headquarters in Geneva, where it was stamped on 3 February 1942. The message contained within the communication, which was limited to a maximum of twenty-five words, was signed by Ernestine and translated from the original typed German:

> Dear children, we are healthy, how are you? Give us an answer soon. What are you doing there? Give us your address.
>
> Greetings, your parents.

The letter was signed solely by Ernestine. The use of the plurals 'we' and 'us' was evidently intended to convey to the children the notion that Leopold was with Ernestine at the time of writing. The letter was subsequently responded to by Gertrude as follows:

> Dear parents, we are happy and well with your letter. New places, with wonderful good friends. Take care. Write soon. Don't worry. Lots of kisses.

The letter was signed by Gertrude and dated 24 March 1942. Beneath the main body of the text, she included her new address,

[76] Ibid.

where she had relocated to commence her nursing training at 1 Derryvolgie Avenue in Belfast. This address was provided by the Burrows family, who had agreed to accommodate her at the request of the Society of Friends.

One noteworthy aspect of this letter is that it was somehow returned a second time to Belfast from Vienna, which is why we have it today. Additionally, it has been folded twice, forming a square, and is identical in size to the photograph of Ernestine if it had been folded along the crease that marked the image. Another distinctive feature of this letter, which distinguishes it from the similar correspondence sent from Vienna, is the address provided for the sender. Instead of Streffleurgasse 4, which is used for all other correspondence, the address is typed as Zrinyigasse 48, in the 20th District of Vienna.

It appears that Ernestine managed to include the photograph taken of her by Karl Piekarowitz, effectively wrapped in the official ICRC letter, hence the folds in both documents. The inclusion of photographs along with ICRC material was forbidden. It is believed that the sending of this particular ICRC document was carried out in such a way as to convey Ernestine's 'proof of life' photograph. The address at Zrinyigasse 48, as far as can be ascertained, had no connection to the Kessler or Schrekinger families. On street directories of Vienna for the years either side of 1942 the property is recorded as being 'vacant' with occupancy only recorded from 1948 onwards; today the address is within an area of industrial and commercial use. The property is situated roughly half a mile away from Rauscherstrasse 4, Karl Piekarowitz's studio. The significance of this address and the details of how the photograph was sent from Nazi-controlled Vienna remains a mystery to this day. It could have been that Karl Piekarowitz had control of the property at Zrinyigasse, perhaps as a storage facility for his business, or maybe it was derelict. Ernestine had to have access to it in order to recover Gertrude's reply with, importantly, her new address in Belfast although she would have been foolish to risk walking there to check for a delivery herself; it makes more sense that the address was of some significance to Karl.

Once the original ICRC document was recovered from Zrinyigasse, the sending of the photograph presented further problems as it could not have been sent via the ICRC system. One theory is that Karl Piekarowitz sent the photo, folded within the ICRC form to a third party who in turn used the address information on the form to forward it on again to Belfast. In researching Piekarowitz photographs it is apparent that he had clients with connections in Spain and Switzerland going back many years before 1942; a number of his "postcard" portrait photographs have come up for sale recently on internet web sites aimed at collectors of vintage photographs. Some of these items are being sold from countries outside Austria.

There is evidence that a number of secure postal 'PO Box' addresses were set up in both Spain and Switzerland, acting as mail forwarding services during the war years. One in particular was set up under the cover of the Thomas Cook travel agency. Generally, however, those facilities also forbade the sending of photographs.[77] One theory on how the photograph was sent to Northern Ireland is that it was folded and 'wrapped' within the ICRC document and sent via a secure PO Box. The wrapping of the photograph within the ICRC form may have been enough to conceal it from a censor's eye. Another theory is that Karl Piekarowitz used his contacts outside Austria to forward the letter.

However it was carried out, the precise method employed by Ernestine to transmit the photograph from Austria without compromising her safe address and the identity of her rescuer remain enigmatic. What we do know is that the photograph within its returned ICRC document did make it back to Northern Ireland simply because the family are in possession of it today.

---

[77] *Fleeing From The Führer: a postal history of refugees from the Nazis*, Charmain Brinson & William Kaczynski, The History Press, 2011, ISBN 9780752461953.

What is evident is that Gertrude and Fritz received the letter, returned to them within the folded ICRC document, and subsequently viewed the photograph of their mother. This discovery undoubtedly brought them solace, knowing that she was well, while simultaneously eliciting amusement at the absurdity of their father's decision not to pose for the photograph. Receiving the image provided some temporary closure, enabling them to move forward with their lives, grappling with the challenges of growing up in a foreign land without the guidance of their parents.

In a similar vein, the existence of the photograph provides us with a literal snapshot of Ernestine's early days in hiding. Regrettably, we lack any other information from which to draw conclusions about how she survived her time living undercover in Vienna. A third and final communication was sent from Vienna. On this occasion it was in reply to a letter that was again sent using the ICRC Message Bureau by Gertrude on 12 May 1942, addressed to her mother at the Streffleurgasse 4 address, not the Zrinyigasse 48 address which featured in the previous message. Using the allowed twenty-five words Gertrude wrote:[78]

> Dearest parents, Fritz and I are happy and healthy. Haven't heard from you in a long time. Waiting anxiously for message. New place wonderful … many thousands of kisses.

Gertrude again included her new address at 1 Derryvolgie Avenue, Belfast in the main body of this message. The letter was stamped as having been received at the German Red Cross on 20 June 1942. It was replied to and returned on 31 July 1942. The return message was typewritten and without a handwritten signature, it read simply:

[78] Warmington Family collection.

> Dear children, we are healthy. Don't worry. We're fine. Stay good and healthy. Write where you are. A thousand kisses.

The message was signed off in type with 'Your parents'.

The use of plurals in this short message was obviously once more designed to create the impression that both parents were together. The fact that the reply was typewritten indicates that Ernestine had access to a typewriter, perhaps as part of Karl Piekarowitz's business equipment. The lack of a signature on this occasion may indicate that Ernestine perhaps did not have full freedom while in hiding within the Rauscherstrasse apartment and that the receiving and replying to this letter was handled by Karl alone.

Arrests and deportations continued with the Gestapo targeting families and individuals from the streets around Rauscherstrasse; the risk of detection was never far away. We can only assume that Karl Piekarowitz continued with his daily routine as if there was nothing out of the ordinary, although in reality he carried a heavy burden, constantly tormented by the thought that if Ernestine had lost her resolve and broken cover from her self-imposed imprisonment, either through accident or with intent, the game would very much be up.

No further messages were sent from Vienna by Ernestine; a short time after this final message was received by Gertrude access to the ICRC Message Bureau was denied to Jews and the facility shut down.

***

Approximately a kilometre away from Ernestine's concealed location close to the Augarten Park, Helene König continued her existence in hiding with her friend Lucie Munk. The circumstances for her were undoubtedly more arduous. Unlike Ernestine, these two women lacked the luxury of an attached business premises with additional space, a separate stairway and exit. Furthermore, several of the nearby apartment blocks were used as *Sammelwohnungen*, or collecting apartments, where Jewish families were concentrated prior to deportation. Approximately 340 individuals were relocated into and subsequently deported from the short section of street surrounding Helene König's 'safe house' at Blaumergasse 24 in 1941 and 1942 alone.[79] The area was a hub of Gestapo activity which only exacerbated the challenges of attempting to remain concealed.

There is evidence suggesting that Helene König attempted to establish contact with her husband and her daughter Felicitas during her period of hiding. Regrettably, she discovered that her husband Jakob, last known to have been with relatives in Prague, had been murdered by the SS somewhere in occupied Poland; she was unable to obtain any information at all regarding the whereabouts of Felicitas, who was approximately 10 years old at the time.

As time passed Ernestine and Helene managed to maintain their cover for the whole of 1943 and into 1944, a remarkable feat of determination and endurance. From 1944 onward, Vienna fell within range of Allied long-range bombers, flying from newly-established bases on the European mainland in liberated Italy. The bombing of the city, while undoubtedly instilling hope that that liberation was not far off, presented further stresses for the women. During air raids the inhabitants of Vienna typically descended from their apartments and took shelter in the cellars beneath. This refuge was of course denied to those living in the city as *U-Boote,* forced to sit out the raids above ground, unable to hide among others who would question their identity.

Vienna was bombed on a total of fifty-two occasions, both by day and night, with the main target being the railway marshalling yards at Floridsdorf and the oil storage facilities at Kagran and Lobau on the east bank of the Danube. The air raids destroyed an estimated 1,200 buildings, rendering many people homeless.

---

[79] https://www.memento.wien/map/ (Blaumergasse 24) Accessed 16/5/2025.

On an unknown date in November 1944 Helene König's luck ran out. The Gestapo raided the apartment at Blaumergasse 24 and discovered her hiding there. She was arrested along with Lucie Munk and both women were taken to the Morzinplatz Gestapo Headquarters. There they were questioned and detained for three months. On 20 March 1945 Lucie Munk was released from custody and returned to her home. Helene König, having been sentenced to be detained in protective custody, was boarded onto transport train number IV/17 along with ten other women and taken to the Theresienstadt concentration camp north of Prague in what was then known as Czechoslovakia

CHAPTER 8

KZ Theresienstadt - KZ Verband

Theresienstadt concentration camp, also known as *KZ Theresienstadt* or Terezín, held a distinctive position within the Nazi concentration camp system. Constructed in the late 1780s, Theresienstadt served as a fortified, self-sustaining defensive garrison town spanning both sides of the River Eger near Leitmeritz, which in turn spanned the River Elbe some forty miles north of Prague. The smaller part of the Terezín fortress, on the eastern bank of the Eger, was known as the Small Fortress. The garrison was never used in combat, resulting in its preservation as an intact building by 1939. Following the Nazi invasion of Czechoslovakia in March 1939 the fortress, which was designed to accommodate a garrison of 3,500 troops within barracks and provide civilian living quarters for an additional

3,700 civilians in 219 houses, housed a Wehrmacht garrison while the Small Fortress became a Gestapo prison.[80]

Following the Wannsee Conference in January 1942, Reinhard Heydrich, the architect of the Final Solution to the Jewish Question, re-assessed Terezín's potential as an ideal ghetto. The location was deemed suitable to house between 50,000 and 60,000 Jews, particularly the elderly, severely wounded, and Jewish Great War veterans.

Terezín was conceived and operated by the Nazis as a model ghetto, serving as a staging point for individuals destined for extermination in camps further east. Although gas chambers were never installed there, the methods of killing employed were prolonged but equally effective, involving starvation, disease, fever and exposure to harsh natural conditions. Between 1942 and 1945 an estimated 23 per cent of camp inmates perished at Theresienstadt, in addition to the approximately 114,000 souls who passed through its gates and were subsequently transported on to the death camps of Auschwitz and those in the Lublin district of Poland, Belorussia and the Baltic States. The survival rate for these individuals was a mere 2.5 per cent.[81]

On 20 March 1945 Helene König and her ten latest travelling companions, all women from Vienna, arrived in Theresienstadt. Helene and the other ten arrivals were, however, detained in the Small Fortress Gestapo prison, usually reserved for political prisoners and generally recognised as a prison from which few people ever returned. On this occasion, her detention there, combined with historically fast-moving events outside the ghetto along with a timely, unexpected reunion with an old friend, helped to save her life.

Ten days after Helene was transported out of Vienna and interned at Theresienstadt, elements of the Soviet army entered Nazi-occupied Austria following an advance through Hungary

[80] United States Holocaust Memorial Museum, https://encyclopedia.ushmm.org/content/en/article/theresienstadt.
[81] Ibid.

and found themselves just fifty miles from Vienna. The German 6. *Panzerarmee* (6th Panzer Army) led by SS-Oberstgruppenführer Josef 'Sepp' Dietrich, in retreat and much depleted from fighting both defensive and offensive battles against the Red Army in Hungary, was ordered by Hitler to hold 'Fortress Vienna' at all costs.[82] At that time 6th Panzer Army consisted of elements of the most battle-hardened and fanatical Nazi SS units, many of whom had fought in Normandy, the Ardennes and then in the defence of Budapest in Hungary. By 1945, aside from any military achievements made in battle, their commanders and men had catalogued a long list of atrocities, notably mass murders of civilians and prisoners of war, which were added to their regimental histories akin to shameful, disgraceful battle honours. From early April 1945 those troops began to set up defensive fighting positions within the city of Vienna.

At 7:30am on 6 April 1945 Ernestine Kessler, concealed in the apartment of Karl Piekarowitz at Rauscherstrasse 4 in the 20th District of Vienna, would have been awakened by the tumultuous sounds of Soviet artillery fire directed at the German positions within the city. Once more, Ernestine faced the daunting prospect of enduring this latest onslaught of steel above ground, while the security of the cellars beneath the building remained denied to her as a means of protection from the relentless fighting armies that traversed the city streets. By the evening of the 6th the Nazi defenders had been compelled to retreat into defensive enclaves, particularly in the districts surrounding the Prater Park and Floridsdorf Bridge.

On the night of the 6th the Soviets took advantage of a lull in fighting to broadcast loudspeaker messages to the civilian population, orchestrated by Marshal Fyodor Tolbukhin. If Ernestine had heard the message booming through the night, amidst the sporadic small arms fire and artillery, it may have

---

82

https://warfarehistorynetwork.com/article/a-soviet-red-army-victory-at-vienna. Accessed 12/5/2025.

instilled in her a glimmer of hope that her freedom was imminent. The broadcast announced:[83]

> The retreating German troops intend to transform Vienna into a battlefield, akin to the destruction they inflicted upon Budapest. Vienna and its inhabitants are now under the threat of similar devastation and terror. Citizens of Vienna – lend your assistance to the Red Army in liberating the capital of Austria; contribute to the liberation of your country from the oppressive rule of the Fascist German regime!

Indeed, it was reported that civilians donned red-and-white armbands, the Austrian national colours, and aided the Soviet forces in the already occupied areas by transporting ammunition and supplies. White flags were draped from the windows of apartment buildings, replacing the swastika flags that once adorned them. An element of the population actively participated in guiding the Soviet troops through the city streets.

The battle for Vienna persisted until 12 April with the SS troops gradually retreating into increasingly isolated pockets of resistance. The main command and control position was established around Floridsdorf Bridge. A directive was issued from the German Supreme Headquarters (OKW), signed by Field Marshal Wilhelm Kietel, commander of the OKW, SS chief Heinrich Himmler and Hitler's personal secretary Martin Bormann. The directive demanded the unwavering defence of crucial communication centres to the utmost extent. The appointed commanders on the ground were responsible personally for implementing this order and any failure or defiance of their duties would result in their execution.

Despite the OKW directive issued at 4:00pm on the 13th, Sepp Dietrich, at risk of having what was left of his army

[83] Ibid.

encircled, ordered the SS to withdraw from Vienna. At midnight the remnants of 3rd and 4th regiments of 2nd *Das Reich* Panzer Division withdrew from their Floridsdorf bridgehead and detonated explosive charges placed on the structure before joining what remained of 6th Panzer Army in a retreat from the city. The Red Army had liberated Vienna. Approximately 37,000 soldiers and an additional 3,000 civilians lost their lives in the operations to both capture and defend the city. Remarkably, Ernestine Kessler survived the battle hiding at Rauscherstrasse. On 14 April 1945 she awoke to freedom in a partially destroyed city, emerging from her hiding place to eventually confront those who would have previously denounced her. She was then faced with the challenging task of finding the remnants of her family.

Two days later, on the 16th, the Soviet Army had advanced into positions surrounding the German capital, Berlin. Ernestine's sister, Anna, the 'aunt' who had once babysat Gertrude in Vienna, had previously relocated to Berlin in 1933 after marrying a German woodworker and carpenter named Heinrich Bucki. They resided at Raüpachstrasse in the northwestern suburb of the city, where Heinrich continued his carpentry business.

In late 1944, under pressure from the advancing Allied forces and as part of the Nazi regime's implementation of total war, Heinrich, having been previously exempted from military service due to his profession, was conscripted into the Volkssturm, an ill-equipped and hastily assembled citizen army comprising tradesmen such as Heinrich, men too old for military service, and young Hitlerjugend members.

During the battle for Berlin in April 1945 Heinrich Bucki was deployed to defensive positions in the town of Ramsin, on the southwestern outskirts of the city. At that time elements of the United States 104th Division, experienced, well-equipped and battle-hardened after fighting their way across northwest europe, were advancing towards his position.

According to their war diary, on D-plus-315 the 87th Company Chemical Mortar Battalion had cleared opposition at Ramsin and established a command post in the town. Faced with formidable resistance, the defensive action undertaken by the Volkssturm units there proved to be severely inadequate. Heinrich Bucki was recorded as having been 'Killed in action – missing' at 10:00am on 17 April at Ramsin. No further details regarding the circumstances of his death are known and his body was never recovered.

From January 1945, in addition to frantically attempting to find resources and bolster defences, the Nazis continued in their efforts to attempt to cover up evidence of the atrocities carried out in the concentration camps as they faced liberation by advancing Allied forces. Camp populations were evacuated and moved under deplorable conditions away from the encroaching front lines, initially by uncovered railway wagons and then, when railway transport was prioritised for troop movement, by forced marches, known now as 'death marches'.

On 9 April 1945, while Ernestine Kessler was sheltering from the battle for Vienna, her Transport No.4 travel companion, passenger number 938 Dr Friedrich Forster was moved by train once again, this time from Flossenbürg concentration camp, where he had been detained for ten months, to Dachau. Each move and re-concentration of already ill and emaciated prisoners increased the spread of disease and death. Dr Forster continued to attempt to contain the spread of disease among the population around him with no resources in an overcrowded camp when, just days later, on 23 April, he was moved once again along with 1,700 camp inmates by train and then by forced march. He described the journey:[84]

> On the 23rd of April all the Jews of Dachau, approximately 1700, were taken away and we

[84] United States Holocaust Memorial Museum: Dr Friedrich Walter Forster collection, Accession Number: 2007.313

> travelled via Neuwald, Scharmitz then Seefeld in a four-day trip. The destination was SS camp in Oertz in Tyrol where, I presumed, we were to be exterminated. A bombing of the railroad tracks made it impossible for the trip to continue. During a try to go on foot over the Karwendel Mountains to Oertz came the news of capitulation. We returned to Seefeld from there the train took us to Scharmitz and from there by foot under great pressure we went to Garmisch-Partenkirchen. While underway to Seefeld many of the weakest died. Many also died on the return trip to Mittenwald and Garmisch where we arrived on the 1st May in deep snow. At the departure from Dachau, when we already were sitting in the train, the rest of the prisoners from the camp Hessbruck arrived on foot. They had marched approximately 8-10 days. I myself arrived in Garmisch in the condition of a beggar.

On the day after Dr Forster's transportation from Dachau camp began, his former colleague and Transport No.4 companion Paul Messinger arrived in Theresienstadt where he joined a swelling population of over 30,000 people gripped by a seemingly uncontrollable typhoid epidemic. Paul, under great pressure, was immediately forced into medical action to try to help quell the outbreak. In the days that followed some 3,000 people died of the disease including forty doctors, nurses and medical orderlies who lost their lives attempting to isolate and treat the population, relying only on medical knowledge and their experiences of dealing with disease in other camps with practically no resources, equipment or drugs.

Six days later, on 30 April 1945, deep within the Führerbunker in Berlin, surrounded by the advancing Red Army, Adolf Hitler, having previously killed his beloved dog Blondi to test the potency of the poison given to him, watched on as his wife of forty hours Eva Braun committed suicide by biting down on a cyanide capsule. He then shot himself through the right temple using a Walther PPK pistol. Spared from the potential torment of capture and trial by the Soviet forces, he chose the cowardly path of avoiding accountability for the devastation wrought upon Europe, the loss of millions of lives and the hardships endured by those who survived.

A few days later, on 5 May 1945, the Theresienstadt Commandant, Karl Rahm, fled the camp, issuing orders to his SS guards to evacuate in anticipation of the imminent advance of the Red Army. Paul Messinger recounted the subsequent events in his October 1945 account.

> The Russians arrive on May 7 1945. We are free but in what a condition. Hunger, epidemics, every day a few hundred more die as a result. The Russians made me work as a doctor, paid. After 3 weeks I was appointed chief physician in an epidemic department because I had proven myself particularly well. Just imagine. I have old experienced middle European doctors under me and I don't yet have my diploma. But as far as epidemics are concerned, I've had enough experience from the concentration camps. They want to take me to Russia. With difficulty I succeed in being freed. I get a certificate from them (as a reference) and I promise to go to Russia one day. Maybe I'll still do that. I have connections.

On 9 May 1945 the Red Army liberated Theresienstadt, taking responsibility for the individuals imprisoned there. Following Germany's unconditional surrender the previous day, the Soviets entered the camp and implemented measures to address the disease outbreak. Despite their freedom, the inmates were initially held in quarantine until the typhoid epidemic was brought under control.

The inmates of the Small Fortress Gestapo prison were also released but were in turn required to spend time in quarantine. Remarkably, Helene König encountered the trainee doctor with whom she had been forcibly transported from Vienna four years earlier at the beginning of her own harrowing journey through the Shoah.

Helene and Paul Messinger remained in quarantine at Theresienstadt until 7 July 1945 when they were released and voluntarily boarded a final train. The train transported them back to the war-torn city of Vienna, returned to being the capital city of Austria, and no longer part of Germany.

***

In April 1945 the Vienna into which Ernestine re-emerged was vastly different from the city in which she had concealed herself in early 1942. Physically, the city bore the scars of war with approximately one-third of its homes sustaining battle damage, either from Allied aerial bombardments or direct artillery and tank fire during the final liberation battle. Most of the Danube bridges had been destroyed and the general infrastructure of the city – sewers, gas mains and the water supply – had all been damaged. As she exited the Rauscherstrasse apartment and approached the edge of the Augarten Park, Ernestine's skyline view was drastically altered. Two imposing flak towers had been constructed within the park, bristling with anti-aircraft guns. Those towers were part of a comprehensive system of towers across the city, designed to detect and direct artillery fire against incoming aircraft. The towers still stand today, exuding an almost alien sense of dominance over those who walk on the park lawns below.

Initially, the city was placed under Soviet martial law before being divided into sectors and governed by the Allied powers in a manner similar to post-war Berlin. Food was scarce and any form of organisation and governance was severely compromised.

Ernestine found herself in a city of the displaced, those emerging from cellars and hiding places, shell-shocked and wandering the streets in search of sustenance, shelter and lost family. Amidst the chaos, and at every turn, she encountered the haunting memories and ghosts of loved ones who had perished forever.

Fortunately, Ernestine had found refuge in Karl Piekarowitz's apartment which remained intact and morphed from being a hidden hiding place into her new home. In the weeks and months that followed Ernestine was faced with a problem: to qualify for any assistance that might be on offer she had to prove who she was, namely a victim and not a perpetrator. For someone who had taken great steps to hide her identity for years in order to ensure her survival she was suddenly faced with the necessity of having to prove who she was. Ernestine was categorised into a small sub-group of those non-aryans who had remained in the city during the war.

It is estimated that approximately 6,000 people, originally labelled as Jews under the Nuremberg Laws, survived in Vienna at the time of liberation; the majority of those people were regarded as 'Mischling' or of mixed Aryan/Jewish marriage who managed to maintain a fragile protection against persecution and deportation for as long as their non-Jewish spouses remained alive and their marriages remained intact.

A much smaller group were, like Ernestine and Helene König prior to her arrest, classed as *U-Boote* as they had hidden undercover. Studies have been carried out using what documentation has survived regarding the numbers in this category but the total number who were believed to have hidden in this way is estimated at being between 600 and 800 people across all of Austria with a confirmed number of 619 known cases.[85] Of the 619 cases, 367 individuals are recorded as having concealed themselves within the city of Vienna. The majority of these *U-Boote* were concealed by non-Jewish acquaintances, with a

[85] C. Gwyn Moser, 'Jewish U-Boote in Austria, 1938–1945', *Simon Wiesenthal Center Annual* 1985

small number, totalling ten known cases, managing to conceal themselves using fabricated false documentation. It is plausible that Karl Piekarowitz, who had access to a photographic studio, may have assisted in providing a false set of documents for Ernestine, particularly considering that his wife had passed away one year prior to Ernestine's return to Vienna from the ghetto. He may have presented her as his deceased wife, although we are aware that he had taken a photograph of Ernestine specifically for her to send to her children. However, there is no evidence to suggest that this was part of a larger scheme to establish a complete new identity for her. In fact, by sending the photograph within a letter addressed to Gertrude and Fritz, Ernestine compromised the details of any false identity she may have established. The photograph, along with the accompanying correspondence, effectively designated the woman pictured as Ernestine. Had the communication been intercepted, the deception would have been exposed. In the absence of any other supporting documentation, we must assume that she remained concealed at Rauscherstrasse and used fully the advantages of the apartment with its adjoining studio as a hiding place.

Given the nature of the act, maintaining a concealed existence undercover, we may never ascertain the precise number of individuals who concealed themselves in like manner within the city. Notably, as we shall later discover, Ernestine, in a subsequent registration document, did not disclose her status as a *U-Boot*. Conversely, Helene König, who was apprehended in hiding, did later acknowledge her status. Not all of those who emerged onto the streets of Vienna following liberation were victims of the Holocaust and it could also have been the case that Ernestine, as part of a minority of those who were persecuted but survived, was wary of who she chose to inform regarding the help afforded to her by Karl Piekarowitz.

In response to the influx of returning refugees to Vienna, joining those who had remained in the city, a number of organisations emerged to assist with their basic needs, particularly housing, food and medical attention. One such organisation was named KZ-Verband, directly translated as 'concentration camp association'. KZ-Verband encompassed a number of aid organisations that provided assistance to concentration camp survivors, Nazi prisoners and, in general, victims of Nazi oppression. This organisation established offices at Alserstrasse 18 in Vienna's 9 district, which housed their Akionskomitee Der wegen ihrer Abstammung Verfolgten or 'Action Committee of Those Persecuted Because of Their Ancestry'. Understandably, KZ-Verband insisted that all applicants for assistance provide comprehensive details of their past, including their family, religious and political affiliations, property losses and general details of internment and persecution under the Nazis. Given the high likelihood of fugitive Nazis, war criminals and ordinary criminal elements in general attempting to obtain assistance and conceal their past crimes, all applicants were required to demonstrate their bona fides.

KZ-Verband produced a two-page registration form to be completed by applicants wishing to benefit from their services. Completion of the form meant providing answers to questions on identity, background and aspects of persecution and detention suffered at the hands of the Nazis. Before Ernestine could complete this paperwork, she had to be in a position to fulfil a final requirement by entering details on the form under the heading, 'The following three guarantors can provide information about your behaviour in the concentration camp.'

Below this line were spaces to enter the names and addresses of three individuals. Ernestine was tasked with locating three witnesses who could testify or provide corroboration of her recent past and the loss and abuse she endured under Nazi rule. The fact that she and her family had suffered under the regime was self-evident; Ernestine had endured robbery, deprivation, untold mental and physical hardship, the loss of her children and, at that time, the whereabouts of her husband remained unknown to her. She had witnessed death through disease and murder perpetrated by SS-Einsatzgruppen death squads at the Modliborzyce ghetto. After enduring the strain of hiding in Vienna for three years, she faced the challenge of finding witnesses to the abuses she had suffered, a seemingly impossible task, given that most of those she knew and had shared her experiences had either been murdered or were missing.

On their release from Theresienstadt and return to Vienna in July 1945, Helene König and Paul Messinger also began to try to rebuild their lives. Paul's main objective was to finally qualify as a doctor, his final exams and registration having been denied him as a result of the Nazi anti-Jewish regulations. Helene's priority, having already been informed of the murder of her husband, was to track down her daughter Felicitas. As the KZ-Verband organisation would only assist Austrian nationals, Paul and Helene, being originally from Krakow and Berlin, initially sought help from the IKG which had begun to re-establish as an organisation following liberation. The IKG organised bulletin boards where people attempting to trace displaced relatives and loved ones could check postings containing details of hundreds of names of returnees and survivors with their new addresses as a means of contact. Those posts were later transmitted to and published in the New York Jewish publication *Aufbau*. Ernestine scanned the messages for any news of her husband Leopold. Five entries under the name Leopold Kessler can be found on the copies of the newspaper preserved today and, as Ernestine discovered, none referred to her husband. With the absence of a telephone network, her only means of following up on those names would have been to write to the address posted or to call in person. She was repeatedly disappointed.

We know that Ernestine checked the IKG postings as, in July 1945, she managed to track down Helene König. Helene had posted her address on returning to Vienna after obtaining accommodation within a hastily set up Displaced Persons (DP) camp, ironically for her, established at the site of the former Jewish old people's home at Seegasse 9 in the 9th District where she had worked prior to being deported on Transport No.4 four years earlier. Helene was one of around 400 returnees placed within the building; her new home there was one of the many rooms within the building.

The two former *U-Boote* were re-united. Ernestine had an important task for her old friend; they made their way to the KZ-Verband offices at Alserstrasse 18 and Helene made a sworn testimony, proving her knowledge of Ernestine on a signed statement which was attached to her KZ-Verband application. The statement read:[86]

> Vienna July 1945
>
> I hereby confirm under oath that in February 1941 I got to know Frau Ernestine Kessler and her husband here in Vienna in the Sperlschule. We were then taken from the collection point at Sperlschule in Sperlgasse at the start of March (Transport 2) that is 1941 to Modliborzyce in Poland near Lublin and Krasnik. After we had decided in secret to flee on foot from the ghetto because of beatings and extreme hunger, Frau Kessler and I succeeded after weeks of deprivation in coming back to Vienna on foot at the end of 1941.
>
> Helene König
>
> Vienna, Seegasse 9
>
> Concentration camp returnees home, Room 119

Helene had clearly provided an incorrect number for the train transport from Vienna, writing 2 instead of the correct 4. This discrepancy may indicate how long she was initially held at Kleine Sperlgasse in March 1941, as she had witnessed one transport depart before her own. Regardless, Ernestine would have been overjoyed to find her fellow escapee and begin to assemble the

[86] Dokumentationsarchiv Des Österreichischen Widerstandes, Copy handed to author.

witness corroboration she needed for her KZ-Verband application.

One crucial piece of information that Ernestine would have gained from Helene was that their fellow deportee, Paul Messinger, was still alive and had returned to Vienna. This could serve as another witness to her persecution.

Paul Messinger had found accommodation in a small apartment near the Vienna University School of Medicine at Strozzigasse 15 in Vienna's 8th District and had indeed provided the address to the IKG. The corresponding *Aufbau* post can be found in the archived March 1946 edition and may have been published in previous copies. In any case, Ernestine discovered his address and wrote to him at his Strozzigasse residence.

On 17 September 1945 Paul responded to Ernestine's letter, sent to Karl Piekarowitz's address at Rauscherstrasse 4, flat 27. The content of his reply suggests that Ernestine's primary objective in writing to Paul was to ascertain the whereabouts of her husband Leopold. Regrettably, she received devastating news:[87]

> To Mrs Ernestine Kessler,
> Vienna 20, Rauscherstrasse 4/27
> September 17, 1945, Vienna
>
> Regarding your enquiry about your husband Leopold Kessler, I, as a returnee from the Polish transport from Vienna to Modliborzyce (March 1941), share the following with you:
>
> Your husband who worked as a clerk by the Jewish Council there, was together with the other Jews from Modliborzyce, resettled at the end of September 1942 to Zaklikow and from there on a mass transport (Number 1. Transport) moved again. As I later found out, these transports went to Treblinka for gassing. It's therefore with certainty to

[87] Ibid.

be taken that your husband unfortunately is no longer alive.

Sincerely,
Paul Messinger
Wien 8, Strozzigasse 15/18

Although Paul had indicated that Leopold had been despatched to Treblinka in 1945, he would have lacked the means to ascertain the precise location of Leopold's execution or even the existence of Belzec as a death camp at that time. However, through a more comprehensive understanding of the Aktion Reinhard camp histories, we now know that Leopold was murdered on his arrival at Belzec.

After three years of isolation Ernestine finally and tragically learned the fate of her husband. He had been murdered and gassed at a Nazi death camp with thousands of others. She had no body, no grave and no point of mourning. Both sides of her family had been decimated for various reasons; although she was alive she found herself alone in Vienna.

Paul Messinger's letter was attached to her application for registration with the KZ-Verband, along with the corroborating testimony of Helene König. The application was submitted for investigation and consideration on 2 March 1946. One year and four months later, on 14 July 1947, she received a formal stamped certificate stating that her application for registration had been successful and that she was officially recognised as a resident of Vienna residing at Rauscherstrasse 4/27 in the 20th District. She was also in effect, not that she needed to be informed, not suspected of being a Nazi.[88]

Paul Messinger was resolute in his pursuit of his previously denied medical qualification. Despite the termination of his studies during his final year he had accumulated valuable medical experience, saved numerous lives and witnessed the grim reality of death on an unprecedented scale. Although reduced to living

[88] Ibid.

in impoverished conditions and experiencing physical decline, he remained determined to obtain the qualification he rightfully deserved. His account, in a letter to his brother Heinrich in Uruguay dated 19 January 1946, chronicled his final, arduous efforts to secure the medical registration that had previously been denied him.

> Dear Heini
>
> After a long delay I got a letter from you and I'm waiting for a letter from the Red Cross with the confirmation of receipt of both my letters. I wrote again later and still haven't received an answer but I hope that now that the link has been re-established and Austria is again connected to the international postal network that postal services will be better organised.
>
> But now, in media res –
>
> On 15 January (as planned) I finished my last rigour (surgery) and it has resulted in an award for me. A day later I registered for graduation and am waiting on the date which has not yet been fixed, because it's always when – Graduation takes place when there is a decent number of candidates. On average 30. Because I took my exams very quickly (Now I didn't have to think about students or other annoying inconveniences) I now have to wait until the graduates of the current year are ready.
>
> According to Austrian law a degree is awarded on the day studies are completed. As a result I now have the right to call myself a Doctor of Medicine. So I achieved what I wanted. It has indeed taken a long time but I pushed through it, I persevered and I finished my studies. I have set other goals for myself but I've nothing to say about that yet. Now I'm taking a week's break to rest, I'm really quite tired.

But next week I'm going to work in the hospital. To illustrate my recent difficulties I want to describe for you the way in which I had to work.

November, December and January were really cold. There was no heating material. With room temperatures under zero you can't work. So in order not to waste any time, I spent most of these months in bed and only got up occasionally to go to a lecture or to cook myself something to eat and to sit an exam. The bed was full of scripts and books etc. By the way, this way of life had an advantage.

I have now gained weight again and reached my normal weight. My body – that in the concentration camps had adapted to the low calorie intake, now reacts by making better use of the calorie supply available. While other people lose weight, I have reached again my normal weight.

I've relatively good postal connections with the USA and I've already got cereals, 3x2.5 kg, 1x5kg.

But maybe it will get better if the postal connection is direct. It's just the first time.

As always I will help myself now. You somehow feel here that everything is moving forward and you can have the most legitimate hope that one day you can live like a human being. I feel happy myself and I don't believe that there are many people with whom I would want to swap places. I was only sad on New Year's Eve. I declined all invitations for several reasons. I was in the final studies and besides I wanted to spend the day remembering the past years. It was a very sad night.

One thing is now certain and I know that now. I won't be able to stay on my own for long. I'm writing this to you although I at present am neither decided nor undecided. My intentions and company change

> like I change my clothes. My private life is completely subordinated to my so called professional life and everything depends on the available free time.[89]

Doctor Paul Messinger omitted to mention the lives he saved through cunning, sabotage, prisoner repositioning and slave factory management, all aside from those who survived due to his medical skills. Despite never wielding a firearm or grenade, he valiantly resisted the Nazi regime by saving lives, each one a testament to his courage and determination. As a *medical resistance* fighter, he undoubtedly earned his victory against the pervasive regime of hatred.

As 1945 turned into 1946, Helene König, Dr Paul Messinger and Ernestine Kessler found themselves standing alone in a shattered city that mirrored the desolation and emptiness of their lives. They were survivors, but at such a profound personal cost. As Wellington remarked on surveying the aftermath of his victory at the battlefield of Waterloo:

> Next to a battle lost, the greatest misery is a battle gained.

[89] Messinger Family Archive.

CHAPTER 9

Never Again

At the heart of this account lies the historical narrative of one Viennese family, seemingly an ordinary and unremarkable unit consisting of a mother, a father and two children. Their endeavours to navigate a simple life in a European city, situated not far in space and time from our contemporary world, provide a poignant and frightening glimpse into the past. Between the years of 1938 and 1946 the Shoah forced the Kessler family members into contact with people, directly and indirectly, both good and evil, with whom they otherwise would never have been in contact with at all. A core of those individuals went out of their way to eradicate the family from the face of the Earth as part of the murderous Nazi regime. Neighbours and friends turned into adversaries and those in authority abused their power to an extreme in their attempt to implement an ideology conceived by a madman.

Amidst that chaos and madness individuals emerged who chose to stand up for what was right. Men and women faced moral dilemmas and made courageous choices, often risking their own lives to oppose the tide of evil. This work has touched on and highlighted the evil and the good, the list of names whom we know to have had an impact on the lives of the extended family is substantial and runs right from the heights of the Nazi leadership down to the proverbial 'man in the street'. The cost in lives, lost and destroyed, of Kessler and Schrekinger family members over the eight-year period studied is considerable but we must consider and remember that this work represents the trials and fortunes of just one family. During the course of the Shoah, many thousands of similarly ordinary families were mercilessly wiped from the face of the Earth without trace.

Indeed, were it not for Leopold and Ernestine's difficult decision to send their children Gertrude and Fritz on a train to Northern Ireland, this story would never have been known and thus could never be told. The primary motivation for the author's writing was the very fact that the leaders of the Nazi regime made such a concerted effort to suppress any record of their actions; this volume would stand as testimony against them. Despite the difficulty of confronting the facts that have now been revealed, Charlie Warmington, as a journalist, recognised the imperative to tell the story. He found himself on the other side of the pen, becoming a subject rather than the reporter. The characters in the report, the murderers, victims and survivors were, with the exception of the former, his own family members. The extraordinary measures they took to ensure their survival granted him life.

In the weeks and months preceding and following Hitler's suicide and the subsequent fall of the Third Reich a number of efforts were made to destroy all evidence of the Nazi crimes against humanity. Many of those mentioned in this account chose a similar ending as their Führer, an indication perhaps of a high level of knowledge of guilt and an inability on their part to face justice for their actions or face retribution at the hands of their captors.

Heinrich Himmler, the Reichsführer-SS, who had personally ordered the executions of Charlie Warmington's great uncle Anton Vogelsang and his fellow resistance fighters Josef Brenner, Franz Reinelt, Matthias Nagel, Fritz Zwickl and Otto Wehofschitz on 16 July 1942 was captured by Soviet troops on 20 May 1945 at Bremervörde in northwestern Germany. Prior to his capture, Himmler had attempted to negotiate with the Allies and had the audacity to offer the lives of prisoners from Theresienstadt camp as bartering pawns in exchange for surrender terms and immunity. Following a BBC broadcast detailing his attempts to negotiate and save his own life, Adolf Hitler became aware of his exploits and, considering them acts of treason, stripped Himmler of his rank and issued an order for his arrest. In the end, the SS had betrayed the Führer. When he fell into Russian hands Himmler had shaved off his distinctive moustache, was wearing the uniform of the Secret Field Police in sergeant's rank and possessed newly-forged identity documents. He was subsequently detained in various prisoner-of-war camps before being transferred to the British 31st Civilian Interrogation Camp near Lüneburg. During an interrogation and safely in the hands of the British as opposed to Russian captors on 23 May 1945 he admitted his real identity. He was then medically examined by a military doctor. During the examination he bit onto a cyanide capsule which he had managed to conceal during his brief detention, collapsed to the floor and was pronounced dead within fifteen minutes. His body was buried in an unmarked grave in rough grounds close to Lüneburg.

Odilo Globochnik, the SS major general, delegated by Himmler with the responsibility of implementing the Final Solution by means of Aktion Reinhardt was ultimately responsible for the murders carried out at Sobibor, Treblinka and Belzec. Globochnik had the blood of some two million Jews on his hands, including the murder of Leopold Kessler. On 31 May

1945 Globocnik was captured by British troops at Weissensee, Carinthia. He killed himself by biting on a concealed cyanide capsule later that day.

Not all the protagonists mentioned were afforded the luxury of selecting their own time and method of death. As previously outlined, Reinhardt Heydrich was assassinated in Prague by Allied Special Forces. A similar fate befell Christian Wirth, the sadistic commandant of Belzec death camp and an operative of the Aktion T4 euthanasia project. Wirth was unable to witness the final days and downfall of the Reich. Following the eradication of the Aktion Reinhardt camps, Wirth was transferred to Trieste in northeastern Italy where, in late 1943, he was tasked with establishing the Risiera di San Sabba concentration camp there as part of SS-Sonderabteilung Einsatz R or Task Force R (where R was an abbreviation for Reinhardt) which comprised a unit of seventy-eight men of the re-deployed Aktion Reinhardt staff. On 26 May 1944 he was targeted and assassinated during an ambush orchestrated by Yugoslav partisans while he was driving in an open-top staff car near the town of Kozina, close to Trieste. He was accorded full military honours and buried in Opicina German Military Cemetery. His body was later exhumed and re-interred with numerous others at Costermano on the shores of Lake Garda in northern Italy.

Josef Oberhauser, Christian Wirth's second-in-command and adjutant on Aktion Reinhardt, who designed and implemented modifications at Belzec which were later adopted at the other *Reinhardt* locations to improve the efficiency of the killing of Jews brought there, was also transferred to Trieste with Wirth. Wirth had previously been promoted to SS-Untersturmführer on the personal direction of SS-Reichsführer Himmler in 1943 for his work in implementing Aktion Reinhardt. He received a further promotion to SS-Oberscharführer in January 1945 on taking command of the Risiera di San Sabba concentration camp until its closure in April 1945. An estimated 3,000 to 5,000 Jews and other political prisoners were murdered there with many more held there prior to onward transportation to the Auschwitz concentration camp.

Following the closure of this camp, the SS-Sonderabteilung Einsatz R were ordered back into Germany where they were inevitably captured by advancing Allied units. Oberhauser and part of his unit surrendered to British forces at Bad Gastein in the mountainous High Tauern region south of Salzburg. Following a short period of detention, he was released and settled in the small town of Bad Bevensen in Germany, ironically not far from where Himmler met his demise at Lüneburg.

In 1948 Oberhauser crossed the new east/west inner German border which had been established after the end of the war. He was detained by the East German authorities and tried at Magdeburg for crimes against humanity. He was sentenced to fifteen years' imprisonment for crimes specifically connected with the Aktion T4 euthanasia operation.

By 1965 the existence and extent of war crimes offences perpetrated at the Belzec extermination camp began to emerge. Oberhauser was apprehended and again subjected to trial, on this occasion by the West German authorities, appearing before the Munich Assize Court in January of that year. He was prosecuted along with five other co-accused. During the trial Oberhauser asserted that he had previously been tried and convicted by an East German court. Verification of this claim was sought and it was discovered that he had indeed been tried and sentenced by the authorities of the GDR. It was discovered, however, that he had only served eight years of a fifteen-year sentence. Furthermore, it was clarified that the offences for which he was convicted specifically related to Aktion T4 as, at the time of his GDR trial, matters relating to Belzec had not come to light. The trial continued. Oberhauser then offered the defence that he was acting under orders. This was considered and rejected by the Court after his friendly relationship with Christian Wirth, appointment as his adjutant and subsequent promotions were highlighted. The allegations against him were corroborated by his own statements made to investigating officers at his previous trial where he stated:[90]

> What Wirth ordered, I had to carry out. It would have not mattered to him to shoot even an SS man if he refused to carry out an order …. As far as gassing of the old Jews was concerned, I could understand it, anything over and above that was too much for me. I thought to myself that there must be some other way of getting rid of the Jews.

During the trial, some of his co-accused turned on Oberhauser when they realised he was trying to avoid responsibility for the events at Belzec. One of them, SS-Scharführer Karl Schulch, made the following statement:

> If Oberhauser maintained that he did not participate in the extermination of the Jews in Belzec, or that he did not see the whole operation from beginning to end – from the unloading to the removal of the bodies – then I say, 'Try another one!'
>
> Oberhauser not only knew well the entire running of the extermination operation but he also took part in it. In my opinion, there is no doubt that Oberhauser was an authoritative person in the killing of the Jews in Belzec camp. The Belzec camp operated for only one reason, and for what Oberhauser did he was well promoted.

Josef Oberhauser was found guilty of being an accomplice to the murder of 450,000 individuals. He was also convicted of five offences of aiding and abetting collective murder in relation to

---

90 'Belzec – Stepping Stone to Genocide' https://jewishgen.org/Yizkor/belzec1/bel140.html accessed 12/5/2025.

150 sample cases. Oberhauser was sentenced to four years and six months in prison, of which he served half. For crimes committed in Italy, he was sentenced to life imprisonment *in absentia*, but an extradition request for this matter was unsuccessful.

In 1973 renowned film documentary filmmaker Claude Lanzmann commenced interviewing victims, survivors, witnesses and perpetrators for his acclaimed work titled 'Shoah'. Edited and completed in 1985, the film spans nine and a half hours and relies solely on Lanzmann's own recorded footage to narrate the Holocaust. Notably, it does not incorporate any archived material.

Lanzmann's pursuit led him to Josef Oberhauser, a former barman employed at a restaurant on Max-Joseph-Platz in Munich. As Oberhauser was working on the premises, Lanzmann and his film crew entered and confronted him. Initially, Lanzmann attempted to engage Oberhauser in conversation by enquiring about the number of beers he served daily. Oberhauser, after reluctantly acknowledging that he had worked at the establishment for twenty years and served 450 litres per day, declined to elaborate further. Lanzmann remarked on the substantial quantity before directly asking if Oberhauser recalled the Belzec concentration camp. From that point on he remained silent and tried to hide from the camera crew in an office behind the bar. Oberhauser died in Munich on 22 November 1979 at the age of 64.

On 3 May 1945 the SS Commandant and guards at Mauthausen concentration camp abandoned their posts and fled in anticipation of the imminent arrival of American forces. A contingent of fifty Viennese firefighters based at the camp secured the perimeter while internal organisation was taken over by an administrative committee composed of prisoners. Two days later, on 6 May, US combat units entered and liberated the camp.

The camp commandant, Franz Ziereis, had fled ahead of the American forces' arrival and was eventually tracked down approximately 100 miles away on the 23rd. He had been in hiding with his wife in a cottage in Spital, south of Linz in Austria.

During his capture, US troops, who had discovered him, opened fire when he attempted to flee. He was hit by gunfire and wounded in the arm and back. Ziereis was taken by the US soldiers to Gusen concentration camp, a Mauthausen sub-camp, where he received medical treatment at the camp hospital. On his arrival, the liberated camp inmates who had become aware of his detention, had to be restrained from attempting to beat him to death.

Following his initial treatment, Ziereis was interrogated by Hans Maršálek, a former Mauthausen inmate and Austrian socialist resistance operative. During this interrogation Ziereis made a confession that was recorded by Maršálek in writing which implicated him and numerous Mauthausen camp staff members in crimes against humanity. The statement, which comprises approximately fifteen pages when translated and typed, provides a chilling account of the atrocities committed at the camp. Ziereis best describes the circumstances surrounding his arrest in the statement's introduction.[91]

> On the 23rd May 1945, about 18 o'clock [1800hrs] I was wounded near the cottage of Irin, near Spital by American soldiers while trying to escape them. My name is Franz Ziereis, born 13 August 1905. I was commander-in -chief of Lager Mauthausen and other camps depending on that camp. I got shot through the left upper arm and also in the back. The gun bullet went through the venter and came out the other side. I had been brought to the 131st (US) Evac Hospital at Gusen and I want to declare as follows … .

Ziereis went on to describe how he had been ordered by Reichminister Himmler to murder the remaining camp inmates as

---

[91] International Military Tribunal, Nurnberg Germany, 13 December 1945, USA Exhibit 249.

enemy forces neared by corralling them into a blocked tunnel, sealing it and blowing it up with explosives. He stated that he had refused to carry out this order. Among the list of atrocities and names of those he alleged were responsible, he implicated his second-in-command, Georg Bachmayer, and included one significant piece of detail that highlighted Bachmayer's particular sadistic method of murder, his modus operandi which, if further evidence were needed, would circumstantially link him to the murders of Anton Vogelsang and the other five communist resistance fighters in July 1942. Ziereis stated:[92]

> The majority of the first few thousand prisoners were killed by SS Hauptsturmführer Bachmayer in the camp Mauthausen. Likewise and even many more were killed by Campfuhrer Saidler at Gusen. The Siedler and [illegible] had the skin from the murdered bodies prepared and made into satchels, lamp-covers, book-covers, etc.

Later in the statement when recounting details of three prisoners who had been falsely accused of theft while working outside the camp he stated:

> A part of these prisoners had been chased into the electric wiring, another part was torn by Bachmayer's dog, 'Lord'. Again another one was sent to Gusen camp for hard labour.

Ziereis, realising that his death was close, requested to write a final letter for the attention of his wife which he was permitted to do. He died of his wounds the following afternoon, 24 May 1945, and his body was placed in the camp morgue at Gusen. It did not remain there for long however before the naked corpse was removed and impaled on the barbed-wire perimeter fence, having

[92] Ibid.

been daubed in paint with the words 'Heil Hitler' along with painted swastikas.

Ziereis' subordinate at Mauthausen, SS-Hauptsturmführer Georg Bachmayer, had little appetite for taking responsibility for his crimes. He fled the camp on 5 May 1945 and made his way to a farm at Münzbach in northern Austria where his wife Tekla and their two daughters, having previously left the family home on his instructions, were waiting for him disguised as refugees. Georg Bachmayer made his rendezvous with his family on 8 May, whereupon he murdered his wife and two daughters before killing himself with a bullet to his brain.

Among the Nazi perpetrators, Adolf Eichmann and Alois Brunner bear the most significant responsibility for the immense suffering inflicted upon the Kessler family and countless others in Vienna. As they perused the deportation list for Transport Number 4, they likely felt a sense of satisfaction as their meticulous plans for the systematic removal of Jews from the city became a tangible reality. Their roles extended beyond mere planning; they were instrumental in the operational mechanics and logistics of .the Holocaust, as Eichmann had explicitly declared at the Wannsee Conference in January 1942, the 'Final Solution'. It is unsurprising that their eventual demise, following the fall of the Third Reich, demonstrated an exceptional level of organisational prowess and logistical expertise.

In late 1944 Adolf Eichmann was deployed in Hungary where, right up to the last days before Budapest was overrun by the Soviets, he continued to organise Jewish deportations out of the city to concentration camps further west. As the Reich crumbled, he made his way into Germany using the name Otto Eckmann but was captured by US soldiers and held in a detention camp. In January 1946 he managed to escape from detention and assumed a further alias, that of Otto Henninger. He then made his way into Austria and embarked on the 'Rat Route', the journey made by many on-the-run Nazi war criminals. He eventually managed to sail from Italy to Argentina after establishing a further false identity, that of Ricardo Klement.

Under the pseudonym Ricardo Klement, he settled in Argentina, securing employment at a Mercedes Benz workshop until his family joined him in 1952. As his involvement during the Holocaust gained prominence, enquiries were initiated regarding his whereabouts. Rumours suggested Buenos Aires as a potential location, until various sources under the control of the Israeli Secret Service transformed those rumours into intelligence and later into concrete evidence, confirming his identity and the location of where he had set up home.[93]

On 11 May 1960, operating covertly and under the direction of the then Israeli prime minister, David Ben Gurion, a Mossad undercover team apprehended Eichmann near to his home and detained him in a secure location nearby. Once under Mossad control, he underwent interrogation, during which he unequivocally confirmed his true identity as Adolf Eichmann and signed a consent to be tried in Israel. The Mossad team managed to fly Eichmann out of Argentina on board an El Al airliner after he was sedated and disguised as a drunken aircrew member. He was flown to Israel, arriving on 21 May 1960. Amid great controversy, mainly concerning the nature of his arrest and the jurisdiction of Israel to hold a trial, he appeared at a court in Jerusalem on 11 April 1961 to begin a trial which lasted until 13 December when he was found guilty of most of the charges put to him. Two days later he was sentenced to death. His defence team appealed the verdict to the Israeli Supreme Court, who ratified the conviction and sentence on 29 May 1962. In a final effort to save his life, he made a plea of mercy to the Israeli President Yitzak Ben Zvi. His plea was rejected. Adolf Eichmann was executed by hanging at Ramla prison near Tel Aviv in Israel

[93] Yad Vashem, World Holocaust Remembrance Center, The Eichmann Trial, https://wwv.yadvashem.org/yv/en/exhibitions/eichmann/index.asp Accessed 12/5/2025.

on the night between 31 May and 1 June 1962. His body was cremated and his ashes scattered at sea.

In attempting to place Eichmann's culpability in a concise context, it is worth considering the comments of the Israeli Attorney General Gideon Hausner as he opened the case against him before the gathered witnesses and the World's media:[94]

> When I stand before you here, Judges of Israel, to lead the Prosecution of Adolf Eichmann, I am not standing alone. With me are six million accusers. But they cannot rise to their feet and point an accusing finger towards him who sits in the dock and cry: 'I accuse' For their ashes are piled up on the hills of Auschwitz and the fields of Treblinka, and are strewn in the forests of Poland. Their graves are scattered throughout the length and breadth of Europe. Their blood cries out, but their voice is not heard. Therefore I will be their spokesman and in their name I will unfold the terrible indictment.

On that day in Jerusalem in 1960, Leopold Kessler, who had been murdered at Belzec eighteen years before and denied even the fundamental dignity of a burial in a known named grave, was finally accorded a voice.

Alois Brunner, Eichmann's primary accomplice and later successor in charge of the Office Of Jewish Affairs in Vienna during the transportation of Austrian Jews, evaded capture and disappeared after the war. The French authorities pursued him *in absentia* and convicted him of crimes against humanity related to atrocities committed at the Drancy concentration camp after he had assumed command there in 1943. Brunner was sentenced to death.

It later transpired that Brunner had taken advantage of confusion surrounding the fact that another Nazi, also called

[94] Ibid.

Brunner, had been apprehended and had been wrongly mistaken for Alois. As a result, Brunner managed to make his way to Egypt and from there on to Syria where he was granted asylum under the regime of President Hafez Al Assad, father of the recent Syrian leader Bashar Al Assad. He lived in Damascus under the false identity of Georg Fischer. In Syria he was embraced by the ruling president who drew on his experience in interrogation, surveillance, torture and manipulation.

Brunner's new life and identity did not go unnoticed. But, despite numerous extradition requests being made to Syria for his return to face sentence, the Syrian authorities continually flatly denied that he was in the country. In 1961 and again in 1980 Brunner was the target of two assassination attempts using letter bombs. In the first attack he lost an eye and in the second he lost the fingers of his left hand. Those attacks were attributed at the time to Israeli extremists.

In 1985 Brunner's cover was pierced by a team of reporters working for the German weekly magazine *Bunte*. The journalists managed to photograph him in Damascus using a camera concealed in a wristwatch and also interviewed him. During the interview he bragged about rounding up victims for Auschwitz and how he personally directed the slaughter of prisoners at Drancy in France in 1943.

Then, on 1 November 1987, the *Chicago Sun-Times* carried a story under the heading 'Butcher in Syria Haven'. The article described how a reporter managed to place a telephone call directly to Brunner which was witnessed and within earshot of a second reporter. The article described what was said during the call as follows:

> Alois Brunner, now 75, lives quietly at 7 Rue Haddad in Damascus where he is protected by round-the-clock bodyguards provided by the Syrian government in exchange for his recent service to train Syria in 'security matters'. In a brief telephone

> conversation in front of a witness Brunner said, 'All of them deserved to die because they were the devil's agents and human garbage. I have no regrets and would do it again.' After confirming he had been living under the name Georg Fischer, he hung up.

Although Brunner was never extradited for trial, his influence waned with the Al-Assad regime, particularly after the younger Bashar Al-Assad came to power in 2000. His existence no longer aligned with the regime's evolving international perspective. It is widely believed that Brunner was confined to a basement apartment in Damascus, where he ultimately ended his life alone and in squalor. By 2014, it was widely accepted that he had died, although an exact date of death is unknown.

***

For Helene König, liberation and her return to Vienna marked the beginning of a further struggle. She found confirmation that her husband Jakob had been murdered but could not find any information of the whereabouts or fate of her daughter Felicitas. She continued to live at the Displaced Persons facility at Seegasse 9 from where she made numerous applications requesting emigration status from the US authorities. During that time she worked within the Seegasse complex, receiving no payment but in effect 'working for her keep' and was rewarded with food and lodgings.

Then, at some point before 1948, she met a survivor of the Auschwitz concentration camp who had also returned to Vienna. All that is known of him is that his surname was Rössler. They began a relationship and were married at Judenburg in Austria in March 1949. At around this time, and possibly as a consequence of their marriage, Helene's emigration application, which up to that point was successful, was closed.

Understandably, with two people who had been forced together following their recent harrowing experiences and each having suffered great personal loss, the marriage did not last and Helene König-Rössler divorced her new husband and made her own way. She moved back to her original home city of Berlin where she found an apartment in the Charlottenburg district in the Allied sector of West Berlin. In January 1956 she made a testimony of her experiences during the Holocaust. The final paragraph describes a pitiful and lonely existence, unbefitting the final years of a courageous woman who, in her own determined way, had fought Nazi oppression. A section of Helene's account, recorded by a third party, reads as follows:

> In March 1949, Mrs König remarried a former concentration camp inmate from Auschwitz named Rössler, but continued to use her first husband's name as König-Rössler. She soon divorced this second husband. As a result of this new marriage, she lost all claims against her first husband, who lost his life in Poland. The little money that Mrs König-Rössler received in compensation for the unspeakable physical and mental suffering she endured, she used to buy clothes, beds and a few pieces of furniture for her small living space (there are currently 6 tenants in the apartment). Mrs König is also ill, is under constant medical treatment and requires non-medical medication. Mrs König never received a penny for her daughter Felicitas, who would be around 27 years old today and would support her mother in her plight, and is dependant on social welfare.

Helene König-Rössler passed away on 24 January 1966 while being cared for in the Jewish Hospital at Iranische Strasse in Berlin. She was 75 years old.

On finally obtaining his registration on completion of his medicine qualification at the University of Vienna, Paul Messinger remained in the city until January 1951 when he emigrated to Israel. There he continued a very successful medical career. Paul passed away on 19 June 1994 in Haifa, Israel. He was survived by his wife from his third marriage and his four children.

Paul Messinger's colleague and fellow Transport No. 4 survivor Dr Friedrich Forster moved to the United States following his liberation. He returned to Europe in 1950 and travelled to Paris by train to meet up with relatives from whom he had been separated by the war. He was collected at the railway station by car and during the journey to their home they were tragically involved in a serious collision. Doctor Friedrich Forster passed away as a result of injuries sustained in the collision on 14 October 1950.[95]

Ernestine Kessler remained in Vienna and continued to live in the apartment above the photography studio with Karl Piekarowitz. Of her extended family all that is known is that her sister Anna, who had moved to Berlin and married Heinrich Bucki, killed in action fighting for the Wehrmacht in 1945, died in Berlin in 1988. Her older sister, resistance fighter Eleonore Vogelsang, remained in Vienna after the war and continued to live at her original apartment at Karl Marx Hof in the city with her son Anton. There is evidence that the sisters re-united and kept in touch until Eleonore passed away in December 1974.

Karl Piekarowitz, who lived for only a few years after the liberation of Vienna, passed away on 6 November 1948, at the age of 68. The man who opened his door to Ernestine had settled his affairs before his death in such a manner that Ernestine continued to benefit from the security of his home long after his passing. Ernestine remained at Rauscherstrasse 4 until well into the 1960s before eventually moving to her own apartment at around a time when she established a successful high-end

---

[95] United States Holocaust Memorial Museum: Dr Friedrich Walter Forster collection, Accession Number: 2007.313

catering business in London. Karl also had it written into his will that his burial plot at the Feuerhalle Simmering Cemetery in Vienna should be used for Ernestine's remains in the event of her death. Ernestine Kessler returned to live in Vienna and passed away on 26 July 1991. Her remains were buried along with those of the man who, fifty years earlier, found the courage at great risk to his own life to protect and shelter her from Nazi oppression. He could have easily closed his door in her face and conveniently ignored the fact that she had ever been there. The simple act of opening his home to her undoubtedly saved her life. Karl Piekarowitz, through the research into this work, is now known and remembered by the Warmington family for his courageous act.

***

For the Millisle *Kinder* who had fled Vienna and other major European cities in 1938 and 1939, courage became a common trait. Thriving amidst the unfamiliarity of a rural foreign land, separated from the comfort of their established homes and the nurturing care of their parents, required a remarkable ability to adapt, a quality that some may believe children possess with greater ease than adults. They were scarcely aware of nor could ever comprehend the perils from which they had escaped and, indeed, knew little or nothing of what they had left behind for years after their arrival. As they grew into adults, many harboured the hope that they would be re-united with their parents and restart their lives from where they had left off. For the most part, although they could never have imagined it at the time, they were alone in the world.

A number of Millisle *Kinder* kept autograph books in which they would invite their newfound friends to write messages, drawings and, as time passed, include their new addresses before they moved on. Ernestine Kessler kept such an autograph book as did Anna Nussbaum whose parents had been murdered after her evacuation to Millisle, her mother Rebekka having accompanied Ernestine and Leopold Kessler on Transport No.4 to Modliborzyce. Anna's book, along with photographs and other supporting documents were donated by her to the Yad Vashem archive in Jerusalem, where they are displayed and can be viewed online. A study of the little book alongside the Millisle Primary School registration books allows us to understand the networks established by the *Kinder* as they morphed into adulthood and learned to rely on each other in the absence of their parents.

The messages inscribed in the autograph books appear as diminutive, handwritten gifts imbued with inspirational sentiments. Their naivety and positivity stand in stark contrast to the atrocities that were being inflicted upon the parents of the authors at that time. When read today, there is no evidence of hatred, malice or fear in the content. One yearns to believe that the children were subconsciously developing emotional resilience to assist them in coping with the devastating news that was inevitably to follow with the conclusion of the war. In a similar manner that this work underscores the intricate and extensive nature of the atrocities inflicted upon just one family, the entries and names signed off in the notebooks allude to numerous additional potential volumes.

One such entry in Anna Nussbaum's notebook reads: 'May your whole life be bright like sunshine. Think often and fondly of your friend Erna Sojfer – Belfast 2nd October 1939.'

Erna Sojfer was born in 1928 and was 11 years old when she was evacuated from Vienna and enrolled at Millisle Primary School. Her father Abraham came from Poland and moved to Austria in 1916 where he set up home at Judengasse 8 in Vienna's 1St district. The building at Judengasse 8 was owned by the Jewish community and operated as a prayer house. Abraham Sojfer was a Hebrew and German calligrapher and a Torah Chant Reader and Cantor there. His eldest son Max was also training to become a Rabbi. Abraham and his wife Hanna had three other children, Hilda, David and Erna. It appears that Abraham and

Hanna Sojfer managed to evacuate their children from Vienna in late 1938 and early 1939, Erna eventually to Millisle and Max into Holland. Nothing is known of either David or Hilda, only that Hilda survived the war and passed away in Buenos Aires in Argentina in 2011. Max initially settled in Holland but, as was the fate for many *Kinder* who failed to be evacuated out of the European mainland, Max was subjected to Nazi persecution once again following the Nazi invasion of Holland. He was detained initially in the Westerbork concentration camp in Holland before being transferred to Theresienstadt on 27 February 1944. One month later he was transported once again, as was the pattern then, to Auschwitz concentration camp where he was murdered on 31 March 1944.

Following the destruction and ransacking of the prayer house at Judengasse 8 in Vienna during the Nazi November pogrom in 1939, the leaders of a Zionist youth and teaching group called Hechalutz, based in Austria, decided to attempt to evacuate their people to Palestine by means of an illegal emigration. Abraham and Hanna Sojfer joined this group and left Vienna on 24 November, making their way to Bratislava, from where it was planned to sail down the River Danube on barges to the Black Sea and on to Palestine.[96] The plan was plagued with bureaucratic and logistical problems and little progress was ever made. Eventually, on 19 September 1940, the refugees were moved by barge and boat to the small Yugoslav town of Sabac on the banks of the Sava river, a tributary of the Danube. There the refugees were held, supposedly to avoid clashes with German national refugees moving in the same area. They were continually promised permission to continue their journey to Palestine but this permission from the Yugoslav authorities never materialised.

In July 1941, following the Nazi occupation of Serbia, the refugees were relocated to an old fortress building near Sabac

[96] List of Jews Murdered in Zasavica near Sabac (Serbia).https://www.jewishgen.org/databases/holocaust/0032_jewsmurderedinzasavica.html Accessed 12/5/2025.

where they remained in concentration camp conditions until 12 and 13 October 1941 when the men, including Abraham, were separated from the women and taken by SS-Einzatsgruppen to a remote location called Zasavica. There, they were all murdered by shooting and buried in a mass grave.

The Hechalutz women refugees were then taken from Sabac and forced into deplorable conditions within a repurposed fairground at Sajmiste. Commencing in March 1942, over a nine-week period, groups of women and children were taken from the camp under the pretence that they were being relocated to Poland. They were transported in vans that had been converted into mobile gas chambers and, as they drove through nearby Belgrade, they were gassed by the redirected exhaust fumes of the vehicles' engines. At the conclusion of their journey at Avala, south of Belgrade, their bodies were dragged from the van and buried in a mass grave. In total, 1,055 Hechalutz Jews are recorded as having been murdered at Zasavica and Sajmiste.

After the war ended Erna Sojfer moved from Northern Ireland to London where she lived in the north of the city and established a business as a dressmaker.

On 11 September 1939 two boys, Walter and Heinrich, with surname Hirsch who had arrived from Vienna were enrolled at Millisle. Although not related, both boys could be linked, albeit one more directly than the other, to Anna Nussbaum. Walter Hirsch had been evacuated from Vienna along with his brother Manfred although the two brothers had been separated during the *Kindertransport* process. Manfred eventually settled in Israel after the war, although it is not known where he was housed in England. Walter stayed at Millisle and later met Klara Nussbaum, Anna's sister, following her stay in Dublin over the war years. The couple later resettled in a hostel for refugees set up in London. From there they eventually married and made their own home in North London. Walter's parents, Georg and Carola, were deported together from Vienna to Auschwitz on 2/3 March

1943. They were both murdered the following day, shortly after they arrived at the camp.

Heinrich Hirsch signed Anna Nussbaum's autograph book with the message, 'Always think of your roommates on the farm at Millisle. Later, think about time on the farm where you have learned so much about life. Have fun with life. Sincerely, Heinrich Hirsch. 13th August 1941.'

Heinrich's parents, Johanna and Julius Hirsch, lived in Berlin but held Austrian passports. Johanna, whose maiden name was Wulkan, was a prominent fashion journalist in Berlin who wrote regularly for the *Die Dame* and *Ullstein Album* magazines, published by Ullstein, using the pseudonym Johanna Thal. Julius Hirsch was a well-known theatre manager at the Deutsche Theatre and also worked as a journalist writing for the Viennese *New Free Press*. The couple enjoyed the high life in Berlin, often socialising with the rich and famous of the city. When the Nazis came to power, from 1933 to 1934 Julius Hirsch lost his job at the theatre. At the same time work for Johanna also dried up, her last printed piece being published in *Dame* magazine in January 1934.[97]

The family then relocated to Vienna, where Julius and Johanna both contributed to the *New Free Press*. However, as with many others, they were once again targeted by the Nazis. Following the Anschluss in 1938, all Jewish editors were compelled to depart. Julius Hirsch secured employment with the 'Central Office for Jewish Emigration' and discovered that, despite its name, the department was merely an SS deportation facility. He frequently found himself in the immediate vicinity of the department's head, Adolf Eichmann. Following the November pogrom of 1938, Eichmann explicitly stated to him, 'If you are already afraid, you should wait for what comes next.' As the situation worsened in Vienna, Johanna and Julius became aware of the necessity of

[97] Hirsch Family Archive, Yael Hirsch, USA.

considering the future of their children, Heinrich and his older brother Friedrich.[98]

The family deliberated over their options, hesitant to be separated from their children. They engaged in debate similar to the Kesslers and numerous other families at that time. Ultimately, they decided to send the children to safety via a Kindertransport to England. The two brothers left on what turned out to be the final Kindertransport to depart from Vienna. During the process, the two boys were separated, with Friedrich settling in Norfolk in England and Heinrich travelling on to Millisle in Northern Ireland.

Johanna and Julius were subjected to the Nazi pattern of deprivation and robbery in Vienna until they were eventually summoned to report to the repurposed school at Kleine Sperlgasse 2a from where they were forced onto railway Transport No. 37. From Aspang station, Julius and Johanna Hirsch, having been forced to drop her 'Thal' pseudonyms, were taken as passengers 330 and 331 to Theresienstadt concentration camp, arriving there on 20 August 1942. Julius perished in the camp three months later on 18 November 1942. Johanna Thal survived at Theresienstadt until 16 May 1944 when she was selected to be transported to Auschwitz along with 7,500 others ahead of a controversial Red Cross inspection. This was part of a Nazi propaganda stunt and deception where Theresienstadt was superficially made up to appear as an idyllic detention facility for the benefit of the Red Cross officials. Upon arrival at Auschwitz, Johanna was immediately murdered in the gas chambers.

At Millisle, Heinrich nurtured an interest in the arts and envisaged graphic design as a potential career path. In pursuing this artistic endeavour, he enrolled at the Belfast School of Art and concurrently engaged in acting. Heinrich made an acting debut in a Savoy Players' production at the esteemed Belfast

---

[98] Ibid.

Grand Opera House where he held a prominent role in Lillian Hellman's anti-Nazi play *Watch on the Rhine*.[99]

During this period, Heinrich began to adopt a new name, a practice prevalent among those displaced and compelled to integrate into new communities. At Millisle, he adopted his first name as Henry before ultimately changing his full name to David Hurst. Prior to the conclusion of the war in 1944, Heinrich enlisted with the Royal Irish Fusiliers, serving in liberated Europe and witnessing the devastation of Berlin. Despite this, he continued to act as a member of an army entertainment troupe. On his demobilisation, his acting career took off with a 1948 London West End debut in *The Perfect Woman*.

From that point on, his career experienced rapid growth, leading him to relocate to the United States and participate in numerous Broadway productions. He also appeared in a diverse range of cinema and television productions, including *Star Trek*, *The Monkees*, *Kelly's Heroes*, where he collaborated with Clint Eastwood and Donald Sutherland, and *The Boys From Brazil*, a thriller based on the pursuit of the Nazi doctor Josef Mengele.

In the 1990s David Hurst returned to Berlin where he continued to work on creative projects until, tragically, he passed away in 2000 due to complications following a stroke. His connections to Millisle in Northern Ireland and his acting debut in Belfast have largely gone unnoticed.

In a letter sent to Gertrude and Fritz prior to the sending and receiving of the ICRC communications, and believed to have been posted before her deportation to the ghetto at Modliborzyce, Ernestine asked Gertrude 'Is Paula Spitz still with you there'.[100] On checking the Millisle records it could be seen that there was a Paula Spitz in the Millisle Kinder community. In researching the Spitz family, it is unclear how Ernestine Kessler knew Paula Spitz. Initiall,y it was believed that she and Ernestine may have been forced together at the school at Kleine Sperlgasse

[99] Ibid.

[100] Warmington Family Archive.

2a or at the Modliborzyce ghetto. However, further research revealed that this was not the case. It does appear that there was some link between the two families with Paula's mother attempting to find news of her daughter through her friend Ernestine.

Paula's biological mother died during her birth in 1930 and her father Leo remarried a woman called Else Gross in Vienna not long afterwards. On 2 June 1938 Leo made an emigration application through the IKG on behalf of himself, his daughter Paula, his wife Else and his mother-in-law from his first marriage, Anna Mayer. Three weeks later, on 25 June 1938, Leo was deported to Dachau concentration camp. He was detained there for a period of three months before being released on 23 September 1938. On 14 April 1939 he was again detained and, on this occasion, sent to Buchenwald concentration camp. This obvious change in circumstances forced Else to re-submit an emigration request to the IKG on 20 August in her own name, including only Paula on the application. Just two days later, as a result of a parallel application made through the Society of Friends, Paula was accepted onto the last Kindertransport to leave Vienna. She enrolled at Millisle Primary School on 9 October 1939.

On 12 May 1942 Else, Paula's stepmother was deported from Vienna on Transport No.20 and taken to the Izbica ghetto in the Lublin district of Poland. Over the period of a week, starting on 2 November 1942, the entire camp population, estimated at around 4,500 people, was liquidated by men from Hans Frank's Abteilung Sonderdienst (Department of Special Services). The prisoners were murdered by being shot at close range and buried in mass graves where they fell; the whole process took a week to complete.

Three weeks earlier Paula's grandmother, Anna Mayer, was deported on Transport No.45 from Vienna to Theresienstadt. It is believed that she was later murdered at Belzec death camp. Leo Spitz's fate is not known; it is not believed that he survived the

Holocaust. Paula left Childhaven in Millisle on 17 August 1940; there is evidence that she settled with a Belfast family in the Elmwood Terrace area of the city; no further details of her life beyond that point are known.[101]

***

Brigit Louise Kelsey, noted as 'Miss Kelsey' in Gertrude's cookbook, was forced to return to England following the outbreak of the Second World War. A few months later, in March 1940, she married her Vienna Friends colleague David Hodgkin in a service at The Hampstead Meeting House. For the rest of the war both continued to work for the interests of refugees in the Friends Germany Emergency Committee in London. In early 1953 the couple emigrated to Australia and were instrumental in establishing the Canberra Friends Meeting. Brigit dedicated her life to the work of the Society of Friends. In March 1987, while visiting family and friends in England, she succumbed to a very sudden illness and passed away on 26 March.

In an obituary published in *The Friend* on 17 April 1987, an extract encapsulates the life of 'Miss Kelsey', as we now know her. Even up to the date of researching this work, her family was largely unaware of the extent of young lives saved by her courageous determination and kindness during the early days of the Holocaust in Vienna:

> Bridget [Brigit] loved life and its challenges. Whenever anyone was in trouble, Bridget was available and ready, and she gave of herself with an extraordinary generosity. Her instinct told her what to do, when to do it, when not to intrude, when to take matters into her own hands, when to initiate and even when to reprove; all in a spirit of love, fellowship and personal good humour. Life, for

[101]Friends' School Archives, Lisburn, Northern Ireland.

> Bridget, meant the spiritual life and she never tired of exploring pathways other than the one she had chosen for herself. As long as the seeking was genuine, she was eager to follow its reasoning and pass on her findings to others. She was known to some as 'The Spiritual Travel Bureau'. We all learned and will continue to learn from her joyful life.

The final entry in her diary, dated four days prior to her death in London, reads as follows:

Turn out the light
Now is the night
Gone is the night
With the dawn light.

EPILOGUE

Gertrude Warmington (née Kessler) married Dr Theodore Warmington shortly after the war. Dr Warmington had met Gertrude while she was pursuing her nursing training at Forster Green Hospital, on the outskirts of Belfast, where he was practising as a tuberculosis specialist. The couple subsequently relocated to Enniskillen where they raised their two children, Charlie and Alan.

Fritz or Fred Kessler departed Northern Ireland on reaching the age of 18 and settled in Wolverhampton. He became an accomplished engineer, engaging in various professional activities and travelling extensively across the globe.

The war and, indeed, the Holocaust had left an indelible impact on the family. Although both Fred and Gertrude eventually succeeded in locating their mother, Ernestine, after the war, the children had matured and their childhood had been lost. Despite their efforts to re-unite in Vienna and Northern Ireland, they discovered that their lives had progressed independently in the intervening years. Each of them had become an individual and was living their own life in culturally different ways.

The children did not learn of their father Leopold's murder at the hands of the Nazis until 1960 and, in fact, as this work has highlighted, never ever learned of the exact circumstances of their father's death, nor for that matter their mother's plight, her experiences in hiding, nor even the courageous stand their aunt and uncle made against tyranny. On the occasions when they did meet up Ernestine spared them the horrific details of the past, perhaps unable to stomach the recollection herself. Ernestine had the courage to save their lives and had possessed the wisdom, as painful as it may have been, to preserve their innocence and not corrupt their minds with hatred and revenge.

The Nazis had murdered her husband, broken her family and put her through untold tortures. Enough was enough.

During an audio interview conducted in 2004 by the then BBC Radio Foyle journalist Deirdre Donnelly, Gertrude's extent of knowledge of events that transpired in Vienna during the war was brought to light. In the interview, which has been partially reproduced below, Gertrude recounts her awareness of matters for which we now possess a more comprehensive understanding. Her son Charlie must now come to terms with what she did not know in the knowledge and belief that it was never the case that she was intentionally concealing the truth from him. He was, and is, a second-generation survivor of the Shoah.

Deirdre Donnelly's questions are in brackets.

Gertrude Warmington:

'I was told that I wasn't allowed to work. And I had to go every month after I was 18, I had to go to a Police barracks and show that I was still here and not doing any harm. Because I was an alien. Austria was at war with Britain and I could have done anything to help Hitler, and that's why I had to leave Millisle because it was the seaside. Apparently people can do things at the seaside. I don't know what but communicate some way, send info.

I had to go to Belfast and live within a two-mile radius. I wasn't allowed out of that two-mile radius. I was like a prisoner. Fortunately, I applied to do nursing, and I was too busy to go outside the two-mile limit.

Up until September, yes I had letters from home. But once the war started, that all ceased. I had Red Cross letters, twenty-five words to say 'Hi' to Mum and Dad. I got several of those during the war. This is from 1942. It only has my Mum's name on it, because my Dad had already been taken to concentration camp. He died. So she has her name. But I think I have one or two when my father was still alive.

[Did your mother tell you your father wasn't there any more?]

No, she didn't. Not till after the war, till I saw her again. She told us what happened.

This was another telegram, addressed to 'Child Haven, Millisle, Donaghadee'. Again my mum has signed that, and we never questioned that. There's nothing in the message. It just says 'We are well. How are you? Reply, please. Make a reply. What are you doing there? Give us your address.' I wrote back then on the other side, and that went back to her again. Giving her what she wanted to know.

[The Red Cross telegram is addressed to Derryvolgie Avenue.]

At eighteen I had to go live there. From there I went to nursing. I had to live with a family until the nursing post was open, and that's where I was for four years and did my exams. I specialised in TB and got my exams and all. How, I don't know, but God was good.

This was during the war years. And the funny thing is, I had to go to that hospital because it wasn't a training school when I entered it. You see, I wasn't allowed to work. I only got a pound a month in nursing. A pound a month! To keep yourself in stockings and shoes. As it says here, I wasn't allowed to work. This wasn't a training school, and shortly after I went into it it became a training school so they couldn't put me out. That's where I met my husband, in the hospital.

The nurse fell for the doctor, and the doctor fell for the nurse. And he was a Quaker, and I became a Quaker.

Don't you think God had a hand in that? We had thirty-six years of happy marriage.

[When the war was over, didn't you want to go home?]

My mum expected that. She wanted us to come home and come back to treating us as children. And we were both married, had had families, it was impossible. You don't … and I felt I was Irish. I could not. And when I did go over, I went over nearly every other year to visit Mum, my brother did too. And I couldn't wait to get back to Ireland. I was, you know, it grew on you. You had to live here. You had to do as was done here. Otherwise, I would always have been an outsider.

[How long did it take you to learn English?]

I just picked it up. And when I really did learn proper … I did my Exams, they were tough. Because some of the Irish girls failed them! I was amazed!

At Childhaven – Some of them were orphans, some of them had fathers or mothers but … we didn't really think we were orphans. I mean, we had parents. But again, we didn't tell anybody that. So, we kept ourselves to ourselves, because we could only speak to each other. They were all from Ireland, mostly Northern Ireland. It was a Methodist orphanage, and I would think that they would have nearly all have been children of Methodist parents but who were orphaned. Either of father or mother or both. We were the only two that came to Ireland. I know there's others that came, some of them came, being

Orthodox Jews they would have come with the Synagogue's consent, whereas we had nobody to send us, only the Quakers sent us on because, well, they're that kind of people that take on those that have no hope.

It was difficult, because we couldn't talk to them. After a while it got a wee bit easier. And then unfortunately the war broke out, and everybody had their rations, and the rations were very poor, and we were growing up children and we couldn't ever get enough to eat. Always hungry. The school had just the one room, and the classes were divided up. This master, I remember his name was Palmer, Mr Palmer – he would take one class and then leave them to work, and it was all in the one room. It was just a little country school – this was so different from our school at home.

[Do you think this was all meant to happen?]

Yes, I think my life was supposed to be like that. I think God had all this for me. I really do. It must be. This isn't all just chance. There is a power above that has a hand in that. I'm positive about that. My brother and I, we wouldn't be here. We would have been gone. We would eventually have ended up in a concentration camp, where all children ended up. Jewish children. And they experimented on them and all.

[Was it very painful to visit your mother, and see how many people you knew had been killed?]

Yes. Most of my relations on my father's side were gassed. Killed and had to go through dreadful things. Some of them had businesses, and you know the way the Gestapo went round just breaking things up, and making them scapegoats. Lost lots of them, lost relatives and friends. And we had a very dear doctor. What we called the House Doctor used to come to the house, and he was Jewish and he ended up in a camp. He was a wonderful doctor.

[Do you wonder what it would he like if you had stayed in Vienna in the Second World War?]

I think I would have, just in the early days. You want to be with your parents. You knew nothing else, but everything was yours in your home and … Vienna itself was my birthplace. I would have gone back if I'd have had the chance in those early days. Again, I was only a child, and understanding didn't come until a bit later. The whole thing, I knew then that there was no chance but what my parents had done. They more or less laid down their lives for us, to let us get out. They could have said 'Oh no, let's not save them.' They could have held on.

[Was there no chance for them to get out?]

The war broke out just three months later. Three to four months later, beginning of September. We were only here four months. There was nothing they could do. So many of them couldn't. I mean, there was no way. The Quakers only take children.

[Visiting your mother — was it easy to connect?]

No. the connection wasn't anything like what we had when we left. No, Mother was more of a stranger, and I suppose I was a stranger too. And then you see, the trouble when Mum came over a few times to us here, and she objected to us speaking in English. It was difficult for us. She was old, and she had lost a husband. She had lost two children. She had nothing. She lost everything. Vienna was bombed – by the very people that were taking care of me in this country. Her country was bombed. That's amazing, isn't it?

By this stage she was getting on in life, she was thirty-seven when we left. Both mum and dad were thirty-seven when we left home. And then we were away. I didn't see her until 1960, I think, by the time things settled after the war, I didn't know where she was. I had a bit of a job finding her, as well. It was difficult to get in touch, because I think she was away. She wasn't in Vienna for some time after my Dad was taken away. I think she was somewhere else as well. She just didn't want to talk about it. I can't tell you any details. She was a broken woman after. And who wasn't? She wasn't the only one.

[What about clothes?]

We demanded to wear our own clothes, and then the orphanage had a uniform, and there we were with our white knee-stockings, which they had never seen, and we'd be marching to church in white knee-stockings and little dress, up here and these bare knees. They all had black stockings on.

We just wore what we had. We didn't seem to grow out of them while we were in the Orphanage. Nobody ever bothered giving us anything. We just had our own things and seemed to be quite happy. I don't think there was ever any problem with clothes, as far as I could remember.

[What did your brother do when you became a nurse?]

He left for England. He had to go when he became 18. He was in the orphanage until he left. He wanted to train as an engineer. We were separated then. He was 18, I by then was 21. Almost 21. So, we were all grown-up by then. Well, I didn't lose contact because we wrote to each other, but we didn't see each other for many years after that. Once he went over to England he stayed there. And worked there.

[It must have been great to have the company.]

Oh, it was. It was indeed. Well then, after the war … Enniskillen is twinned in Beilefeld in Germany, and they [Germans] have come over and I have made a lot of [German] friends there and writing to them. But those are the people that I was going to murder myself. I hated them for having done what they did to my lovely country, and my Dad.

But anyway, by this time I loved them all. They're just my friends now, and the horrible things are forgotten and have left me.

If God loves me then I must love them. Isn't that right? They're just human beings like myself, and Hitler made them into beasts. Once God is left out of everyday life, you become disorientated and you're not a human being.'

***

Anna Nussbaum, known as Chana Gross, passed away peacefully at her home in Israel surrounded by her family on the morning of 7 March 2025, aged 96 years. She had previously been made aware of the writing of this work by her granddaughter Noa.

NOMINAL INDEX

Al Assad, Bashar 197, 198
Al Assad, Hafez 197
Bachmayer, Georg 132, 133, 193, 194
Bauer, Leopold 136
Ben Gurion, David 195
Berndorff, Emil 135
Bormann, Martin 169
Bouhler, Philip 102
Brenner, Josef 123 on
Brenner, Marie 129, 137
Brunner, Alois 194, 196
Bucki, Heinrich 170, 200
Cadbury, Emma 61
Campbell, Mary 61
Dagan, Ezra 148
Dannenberg, Martin 24
DeJardin, Lucie 60
Dietrich, Josef (Sepp) 168, 169
Dolfuss, Engelbert 17, 18, 70
Donnelly, Deirdre 212
Ebner, Karl 81
Eichmann, Adolf 32 on
Epstein, Hedy 63
Feix, Reinhold 143
Fiennes, Ralph 148
Forster, Dr. Friedrich 144, 171, 211
Globocnik, Otto 110, 116, 188
Gordon, Alexander 63
Göring, Hermann 108
Göth, Amon 146
Gross, Chana (see Anna Nussbaum)
Groszmann, Franzi 62
Grynspan, Herszchel 41
Guertner, Franz 103
Hartmann, Siegfried 129, 136
Haughton, Ethel 61
Heim, Franz 117
Heydrich, Reinhard 77, 108, 115, 135, 167, 189
Himmler, Heinrich 27, 110, 118 135, 169, 187
Hirsch, Carola 204
Hirsch, Georg 204
Hirsch, Heinrich 204
Hirsch, Johanna 205
Hirsch, Julius 205
Hirsch, Walter 204
Hitler, Adolf Throughout
Hodgkin, David 59, 209
Hölfe, Hermann 117
Huber, Franz J 28
Hurst, David (see Heinrich Hirsch). 207
Kac, Nanette 86
Kac, Zyskind 86

Frank, Hans 68, 77, 80, 208
Friedman, Hans 70
Gabčik, Josef 115
Kessler, Ernestine. Throughout
Kessler, Leopold Throughout
Kessler, Salomon 16, 36
Kietel, Wilhelm 169
Klement, Ricardo (see Adolf Eichmann)
Kneucker, Irma 94 - 96
Kneucker, Siegfried 94 - 96
König, Felicitas 72, 84, 164, 178, 198
König, Helene 72 on
König, Jakob 72
Korherr, Dr. Richard 118
Kozich, Thomas 35
Kubie, Alfons 97
Kubie, Hermine 97, 99, 156
Kubiš, Jan 115
Kuchmann, Otto 32, 55
Lanzmann, Claude 191
Liposky, Franz 47 - 59
Löwenherz, Josef 32, 55, 75, 80, 92
Maršálek, Hans 192
Matsch, Teresia 129, 137
Mayer, Leopold 133
Messinger, David 72
Messinger, Erna 72, 84, 114, 141
Messinger, Heinrich 71
Messinger, Jetty 69, 141
Katz, Erik 38, 39
Kelsey, Brigit 47, 52, 58, 209
Keneally, Thomas 147
Nussbaum, Noa 218
Nussbaum, Rebekka 74, 76, 79, 84, 202
Nussbaum, Schaje 74, 76, 79
Oberhauser, Josef 110, 188
Oppenheimer, Deborah 62
Patton, General George 25
Perls, Frank 24
Piekarowitz, Helene 55, 154
Piekarowitz, Karl 53, 122, 154, 175, 200
Piffl, Johann 131
Reder, Rudolf 112, 114
Reinelt, Franz 129, 187
Rosenfeld, Ursula 63
Schillinger, Konrad 69
Schindl, Franz 131
Schön, Robert 129, 136
Schrekinger, Anna (Anni) 10, 84, 122
Schrekinger, Berta 122
Schrekinger, Eleonore 122, 123, 130, 137, 200
Schrekinger, Ernestine Throughout
Schrekinger, Rosa 122
Segal, Lore 62
Sojfer, Erna 67, 202
Sowiakowski, Dr. 95
Spielberg, Steven 147
Spitz, Leo 208

Messinger, Paul 69 on

Munk, Lucie 153, 163, 165

Nagel, Mathias 128, 130, 138, 187

Neumayer, Käthe 69

Nussbaum, Anna 74, 201, 204, 218

Nussbaum, Klara 74, 204

Tolbukhin, Fyodor 168

Vermes, Alfred 70

Vermes, Elisabeth 70

Villard, Oswald 77, 78

Vogelsang, Anton 123 - 138, 187, 193

Von Rath, Ernst 41

Von Schuschnigg 19

Wehofschitz, Otto 129 - 138, 187

Weiss, Oskar 102 - 105

Weiss, Rosalina 102

Wijsmuller-Meijer 46

Wirth, Christian 110, 143, 188, 190

Ziereis, Franz 134, 191

Szilagyi, Friedrich (Fred) 66

Zwickl, Anna 129

Zwickl, Friedrich 129 -134

Spitz, Paula 207

Spohrer, Jolante 87, 97

Steiner, Max 106, 108

Sumpf, Grete 69, 86, 97

Thal, Johanna (see Hirsch)

ABOUT THE AUTHOR

Mark Scott is a historical researcher who has previously authored three -fiction publications: *"The Man Who Shot The Great War," "Among The Kings - The Unknown Warrior an untold story,"* and *"We Fought On D-Day - Ulstermen in Normandy in their own words."*

In his latest work, Scott continues to employ his signature investigative approach, often uncovering previously unknown or overlooked historical facts. He is a skilled photographer, having taught the subject in his native Belfast several years ago. He utilises his photographic expertise, typically with vintage period cameras, to enhance the atmospheric quality of his published works.